The Folk Art Instrument Builders Reference

© 2014 Charles E. Atchison

ISBN 978-0-692-31718-1

charles.atchison@gmail.com
http://www.CharlesAtchison.com

The cover photograph is owned by the author and resides within his personal collection of folk art ephemera.

Special thanks to Alex Atchison and Kate Weise for their photography, proofreading and editing contributions of this book.

Table of Contents

Tools **4**
The Cigar Box Guitar **6-66**
   Wooden Peg Tuners **11-20**
   Diddley Bow **21-35**
   Relic Style Four String Guitar **37-66**
   Distressing the wood **42-48**
   Ebonizing **44-47**
   Age metal parts **45**
Tenor Hubcap Banjo **67-131**
      Fret Position Markers **77-78**
      Fretting the Neck **85-102**
      Fret Templates **93-95**
      Dressing the Frets **101-102**
      Tuning Keys & the Nut **103-108**
      Staining the Neck **109-113**
      Attach the Neck **114-117**
      Adding the Jack & Piezo Pickup **118-122**
      String Retainer **123-126**
      Tailpiece, Bridge & Final Assembly **127-131**
Headstocks **132-138**
Kalimba (Thumb Piano) **139-147**
Bracing **148-149**
Wind your own Pickups **150-155**
Wiring **156-163**
Scarf Joint **164-170**
Bridges and Tailpieces **171-176**
Build a wooden cigar bridge **177-185**
Cajón Drum **186-192**
Washtub Bass (Gutbucket) **193-198**
Recommended Resources **199**

The intent of this book is to provide a reference for the construction of functional Folk Art & Roots instruments. This book is by no means inclusive. Primarily because the highly proclaimed first rule of Roots instrument building is that there are no rules. Roots instruments can be constructed out of boxes, cans, hubcaps, toasters, suitcases, cookie tins, literally with anything you have available. As far as string instruments are concerned you are not limited to the number of strings, scale length, number of frets or to even have any frets at all. It's all about having fun, making art and making music. In the pages ahead I will show you some of the techniques, principles, tricks and tips that I have amassed during my decade or so journey of folk art/roots instrument building. I've had many hobbies throughout my lifetime but never one nearly as fulfilling. It's a journey that will connect you with other enthusiasts from all around the world. It's an addiction that might just consume you and it all starts with your very first build.

Charles E. Atchison

Suggested Tools

Hammer
Screwdrivers
Sandpaper
Exacto Knife
Wire Cutters
Hand saw
Fret saw and Fret cutters
Dremel with sanding and cutting wheel attachments
Ruler
Rasp
Hand drill and bits
Chisel set
Numerous clamps, various sizes
Combination Square or Steel Square
Soldering gun

You will do faster and much nicer work if you can also utilize some or all of the tools listed below:

Scraper plane, Block plane, Smoothing plane
Coping Saw
Spokeshave
Outside caliper gauge
Marking gauge
Files
Forstner drill bits
Hole Saw
Drill press
Band saw
Table saw
Wood burning tool
Vise
Belt sander

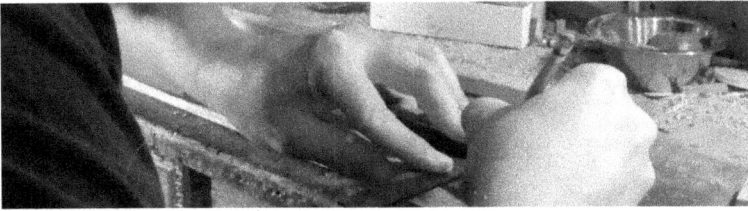

The secret to a great sounding instrument is the wood you use, right? Nope. The truth is, the myth of "Tonewood' is one that will likely never dissipate. Studies have been conducted with expert violinists where it was determined that they could not distinguish the tone of a Stradivarius from that of any other violin. Still debate continues regarding what gives the Stradivarius it's superior tone. This doesn't negate the fact that as a musician one can pick up an instrument and fall in love with it's tone. Wood does not attribute to the overall sound anywhere near as much as the overall construction of the instrument.

In 1995 Bob Taylor of Taylor Guitars set off to prove once and for all that craftsmanship was the real key to a superior sounding instrument. He proved his point by ripping apart warehouse pallets and he constructed an acoustic guitar that sounded simply amazing. A limited production run of this guitar soon followed that sported an inlaid forklift on the fretboard.

Rest assured that if your budget doesn't allow for you to purchase Brazilian Rosewood you will do just fine with whatever materials you do have available. This book is about folk art, yet keep in mind that it is functional folk art. It may not look like a Stradivarius when you are done but there is nothing preventing it from sounding like one.

Try to not lose sight of the fact that first and foremost this is art. It just happens to be the kind of art though that if constructed with care, passion and detail, will become art with a very nice sounding voice.

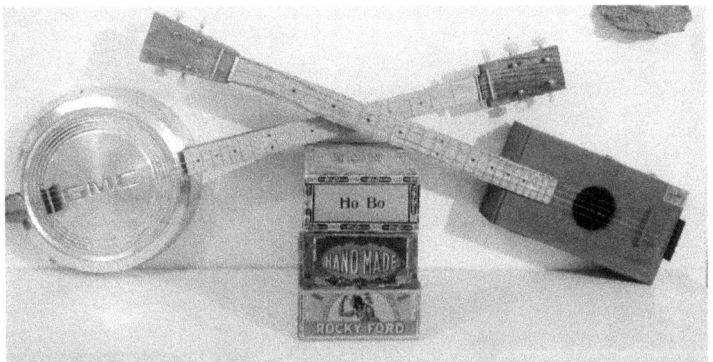

Cigar Box Guitars

Local tobacco shops will practically give away their empty boxes or at most only charge a dollar or two per box. This appeals to the cigar box luthier especially when so many parts can be made from recycled and/or repurposed materials. Many truly fine cigar box guitars can be made for less than thirty dollars.

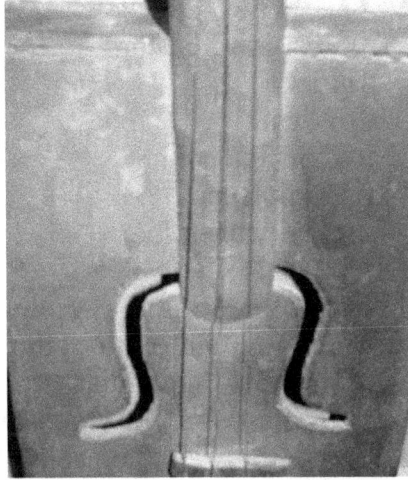

Vintage Cigar box instruments

Cigar Box instruments have been around since the mid 1800's. Artist Edwin Forbes created a copper-plate etching in 1876 titled "Home Sweet Home" which shows a civil war soldier playing a fiddle made from a Figaro's cigar box.

Later in 1884, Daniel Carter Beard published a story called "Christmas with Uncle Enos" that included plans for building a fretless, 5 string, cigar box banjo. In 1890 the plans were republished without the accompanying story in the American Boy's Handy Book.

Before diving into the construction of the Cigar Box Guitar, I want to first provide an overview of a guitars components.

1) Neck	7) Position Markers
2) Headstock	8) Pickup
3) Tuning Keys	9) Wiring
4) Nut	10) Bridge
5) Fretboard	11) Tailpiece
6) Frets	12) String Retainer

One item not listed but worth noting is a sound post. While a sound post is certainly not an item found in most guitars, there are a few archtop guitars that sport them and you'll never find a decent violin or stand up bass without one. So what is a sound post? In essence it is simply a wooden dowel that is slightly wedged between the top and the bottom of the instrument. It is typically not glued in place but rather held by tension. It transfers the vibrations that are normally restricted to the top of an instrument and sends them to the bottom. A sound post can add immense quality of tone and resonance. I highly recommend you to experiment with a sound post. Moving the Sound Post to various areas will also alter the sound. For example moving it towards the neck of the guitar will increase the instruments loudness and render a brighter tone. Moving it down toward the Tailpiece will serve quite the opposite effect. I suggest you spend time moving it all around until you find the sweet spot or toss it out and move on to the next part of your build. Just remember certain boxes have different woods and thicknesses so it is almost always worth a shot to see if you can take a good instrument and make it awesome.

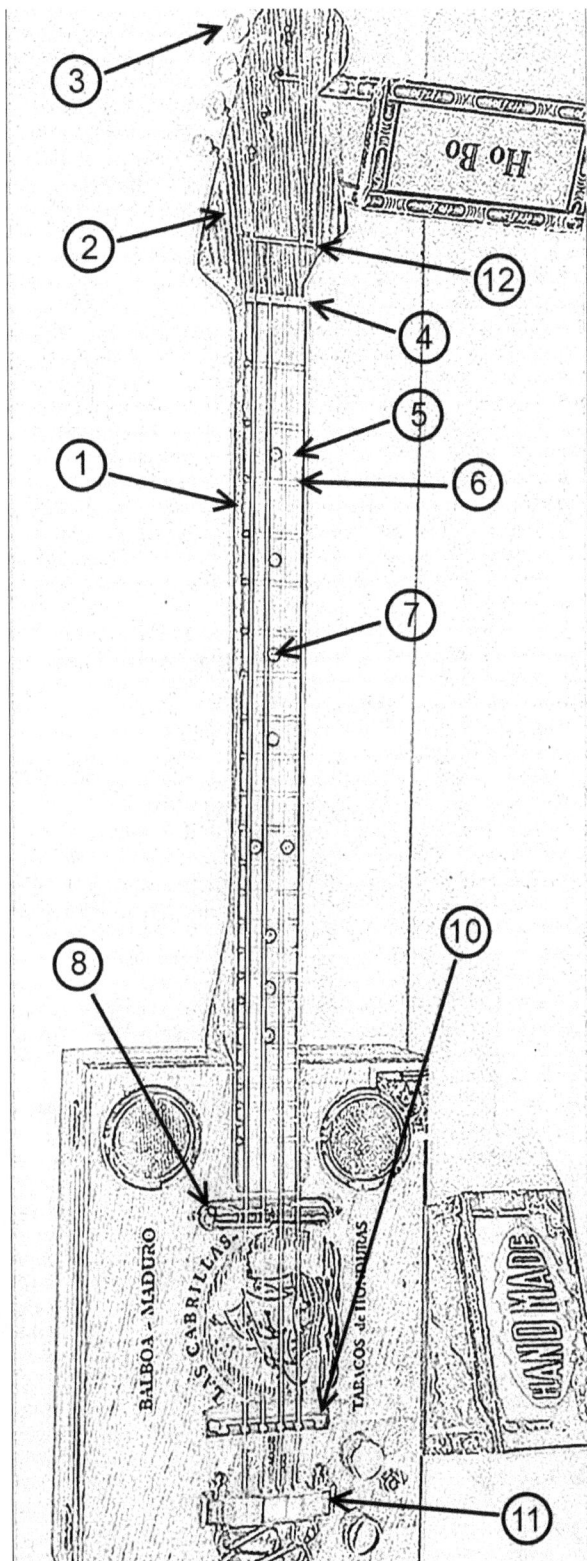

9

So, now you are familiar with all of the components. and at this point you are probably already pondering all of the various potential places where you will fulfill your parts list. Certainly a well stocked hardware store will contain everything you need. However, I am an advocate for trying to stay true to the mindset of our Cigar Box Instrument building forefathers. Poor and struggling yet finding happiness by combining surplus or rather scraps of wood, empty cigar boxes and cheap wire that was often purloined from a front porch screen door. This is where we become a bit of an "Experimental Luthier" and try things that others might not expect but as long as it serves its purpose then I say job well done. For example, in this book I will be taking you through the construction of a Relic style 4 string guitar. The neck was a discarded hunk of pine that I rescued from a life at the dump. The bridge for this guitar was made from a remnant piece of wood left over from another build that could have just as easily been thrown away or tossed in the back yard fire pit. The tailpiece for the hubcap banjo, was made out of a vintage, steel, shoe horn.

Just look around for anything that you can use. Many builders use bolts for their nut as well as their bridge. They work fine. Perhaps carve the nut/bridge from a deer antler or cow bone (wear a mask, bone dust is bad for the lungs). The jack housing I used on the electric Kalimba for this book was built by using an old brass doorbell button. The jack fit into it like it was destined to live inside of it. Just let your inner artist out and give him/her the freedom and the potential for these little artistic miracles.

Wooden Peg Tuners

Consider using these on any of your stringed instruments. They aren't just for Cigar Box guitars. You may just be surprised by how well these tuners work and for an old school look, nothing beats them.

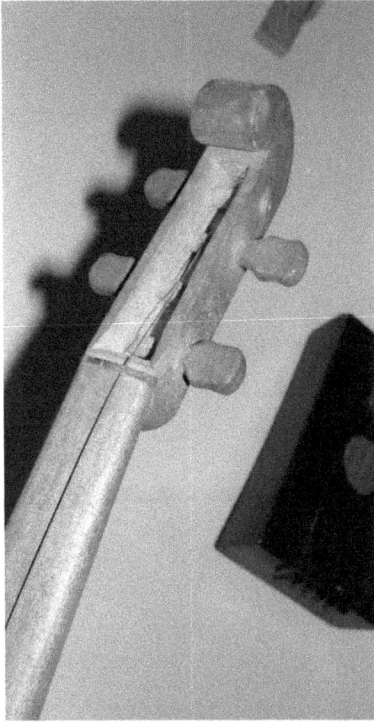

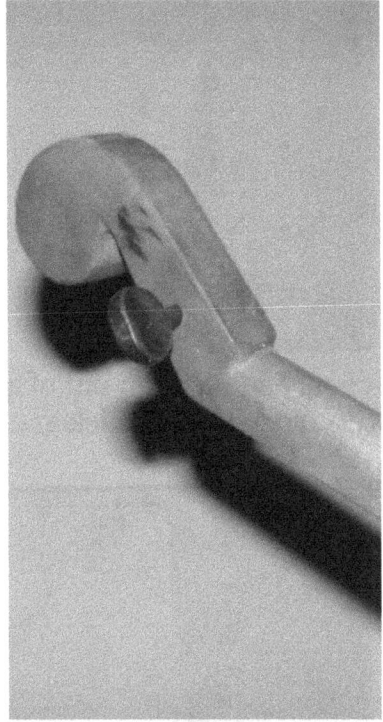

If you have ever played a violin then you are already familiar with wooden peg tuners. The majority of vintage, homemade instruments utilized these as well, primarily because they are simple, effective and fairly easy to make.

I'll make this tuner out of a piece of oak. The dimensions of this block is 5/16 thick and 3 inches long.

Draw a circle approximately 1 inch in diameter.
Draw a line through the circle down to the bottom of the board.

Draw a line from each side of the circle down to the center line.

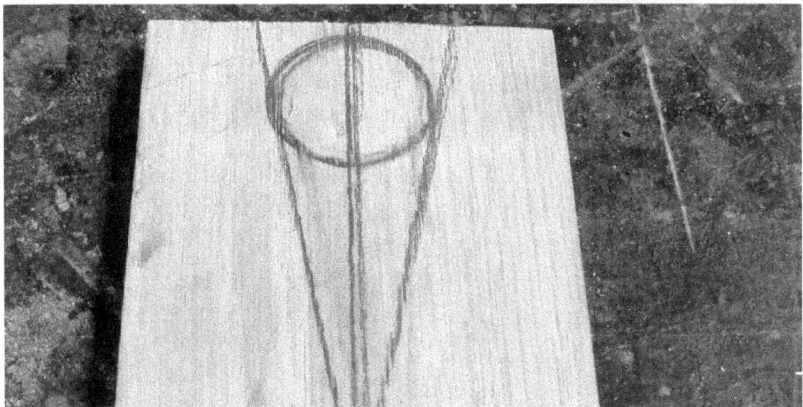

Next, cut the shape out.

Clamp the piece down on a block of wood and use a rasp to round the edges. Don't be too aggressive with the rasp. The first goal is to just take the sharp edges off.

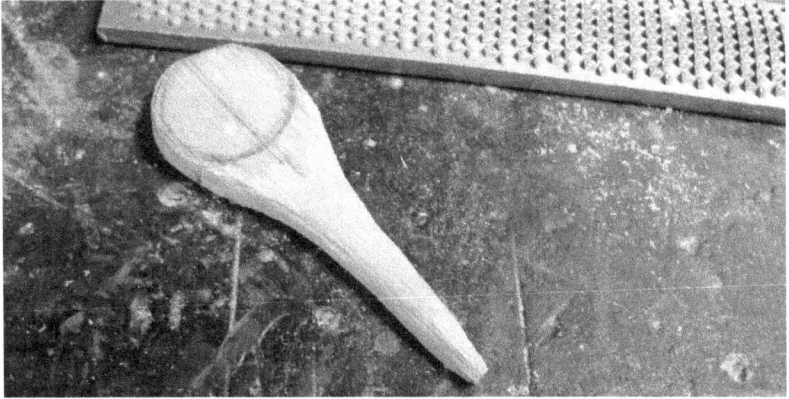

Starting to take shape already.

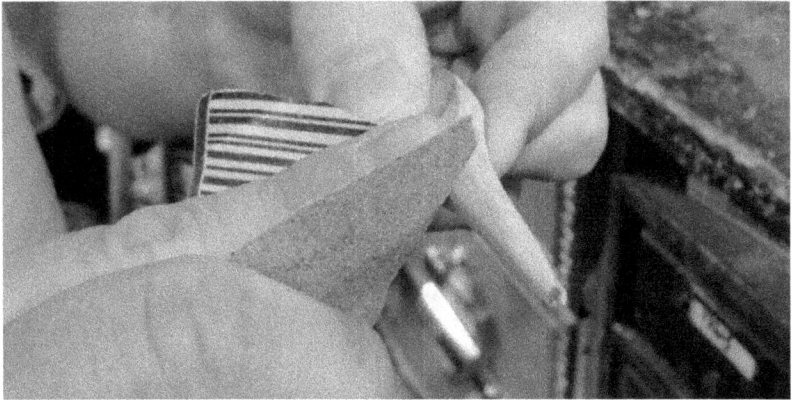

After using the rasp, take some coarse sandpaper and really start to shape and round the tuning peg.
Make a cone shape with the sandpaper and twist the peg back and forth to round and taper it. The taper is very important. You could also use a dremel with a sanding wheel, then finish it off by hand with medium or fine grit sandpaper. Whatever works best for you.

In this example I am mounting the tuner on a one string Diddley Bow (One string guitar). Start by drilling a 1/4 inch hole. Next, from the back, drill about half way through with a 5/16 bit.

The two widths that I drilled will accommodate the taper of the peg and will hold it firmly in place once pressed in and given a slight twist.

Now that it is in the board, make a mark that indicates where to drill the string hole. You want the hole to be fairly close to the neck. This gives me more options when it comes time to make a Nut for the guitar.

Using the drill press, I drill through the mark I made using a 1/16 bit.

It's that simple.

Notice how snug the Peg fits on both sides.

You may want to sand the grip part of the peg more. Some builders carve them out a bit so that the thumb and index fit the grip better. Other than that, this Wooden Peg Tuner is complete.
Notice that I drilled the string hole low towards the neck. The string will be lower than the nut and thus eliminate any need of a string retainer for this guitar.

Diddley Bow

Based on similar instruments from West Africa, the Diddley Bow was the poor man's guitar.

You may have seen Jack White build and play a Diddley Bow in the documentary "It Might Get Loud". He gets right to the heart of the primitive nature of this instrument.

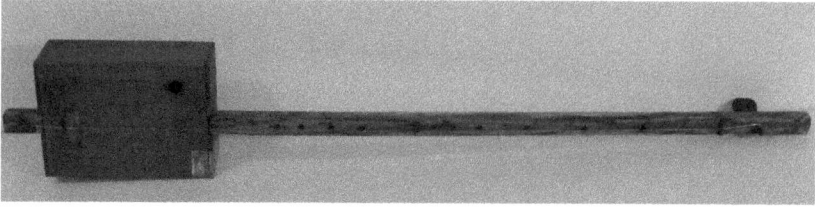

Many notable blues guitarists built and played Diddley Bow guitars when they were young. These wonderful, little, one string guitars can be built out of just about anything.

The simplest of which is just a board, a couple of nails and a length of wire.

If you see or hear modern musicians, such as Justin Johnson*, demonstrate the amazing possibilities of this seemingly simple instrument then it is easy to see why there has been a resurgence in its popularity.

Anyone who has aspirations of building 3, 4 or even 6 string Cigar Box Guitars should start out building several of these. You can make these guitars as simple or elaborate as you desire; fretted necks, fancy headstock's, inlays, pyrography etc...

* Justin Johnson a.k.a. the Wizard
JustinJohnsonLive.com

First, I cut a piece of wood that is roughly 3/4 x 3/4 to use as the neck of the guitar. It is 32 inches long.

The length should be enough to accommodate the tuning peg and the nut and have enough coming through the box for the string to pass through. I am using a 25 inch scale which means the distance from the nut to the bridge is exactly 25 inches. Place a mark at 25 inches so you know where the bridge will be place on the box. It should be somewhere in the bottom third of the instrument.

Using my fret template (**see page 93-95**) I mark where the nut will be as well as the bridge.

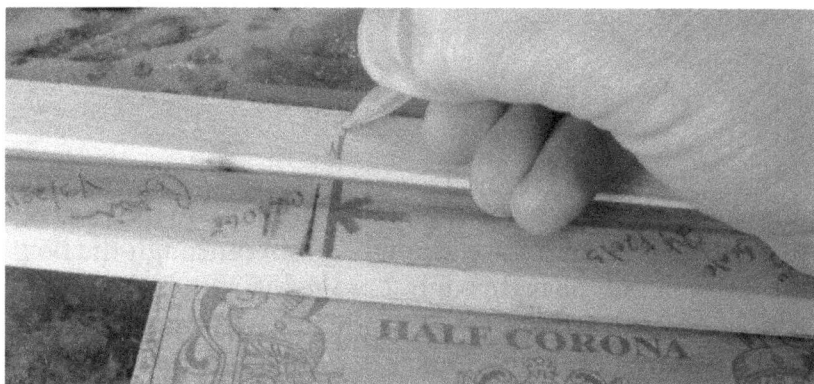

The arrow and line on my fret template indicates the position of the bridge, exactly 25 inches from the Nut.

Next I mark on the neck the position where it meets the box.

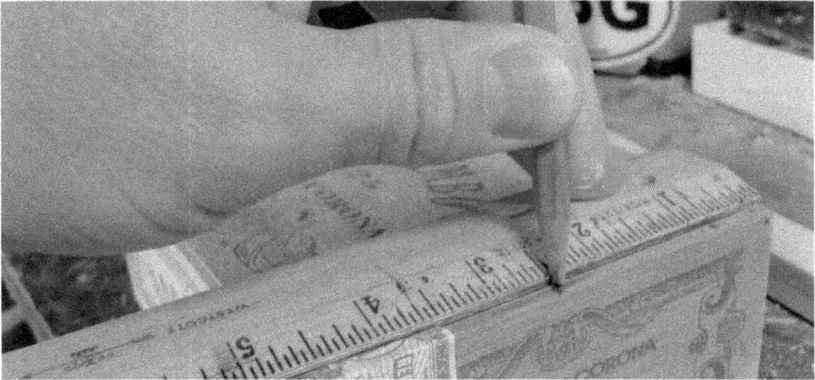

Find and mark the center of the box on both ends.

Use a piece of wood the same size as your neck and mark off where you need to cut openings on both ends.

Important: You need the neck to fit very snug so be sure and cut to the inside of the lines you draw.

I use a hand saw to make the vertical cuts and an exacto knife to make the horizontal cut.

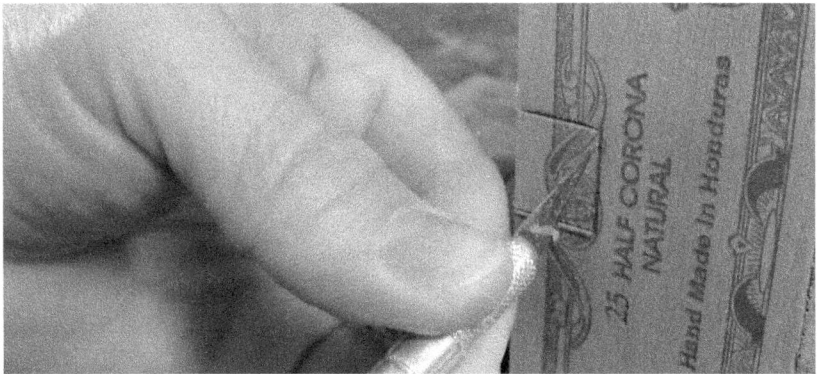

I can normally just score the wood with the knife and then snap the piece out. Be very careful if you use the knife, you may want to wear gloves to protect your fingers.

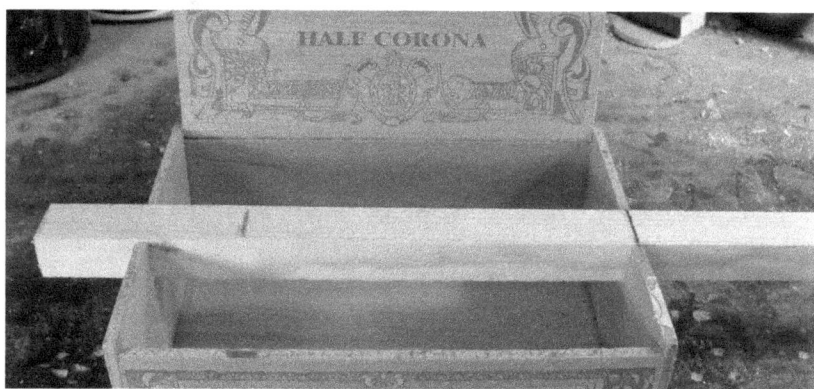

Make sure it fits snug. It's better to cut too little than too much. If you undercut you can use the exacto to shave the sides for a perfect fit. This build is an example of a "through the body" style neck, which is very popular among cigar box guitar builders.

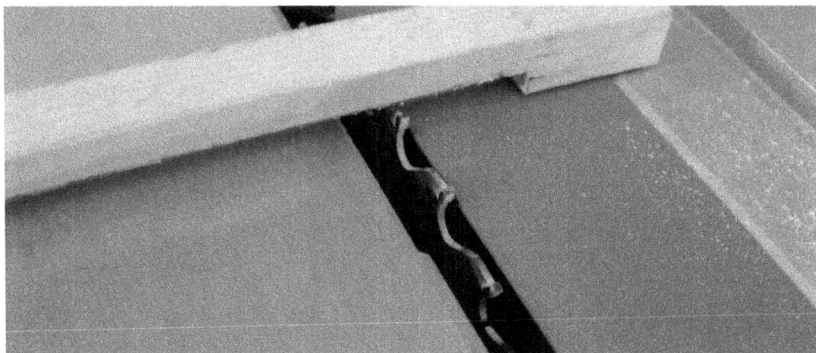

Optional Step: I don't normally do this step for 1 string guitars but I'll show it as an example for other "neck through the body" guitars.

The box will resonate much better if the neck does not rest on the lid. If the neck does rest on the lid you can correct this by making a notch in the neck using a table or band saw. You will still need a little bit of the neck touching the lid just on each side to prevent the neck from wobbling up and down.

You may want to leave a bit on the neck in the area where the bridge will sit, especially if the lid of your box is thin and/or too flexible. The lid on the box I am using is very firm and doesn't require extra support.

The lid should close completely and the neck should not wobble in any direction. If your first build or two doesn't come out just right, feel free to use wood screws or glue or anything necessary to correct the problem. Nearly every mistake can be corrected.

Using the band saw I cut a small pyramid shaped piece of wood to use as the bridge. It is important that the base is completely flat when it is on the lid. The triangular shape ensures that there is a very small point of contact for the string.

Sand the neck. Edges need to be smooth to prevent any splinters.

Use a fret saw and cut a notch for the nut to sit in.

Make a couple of cuts and then pop the wood out with a small screwdriver or chisel.

Sand or file the notch.

Cut a small piece of hardwood to use as the nut. It should fit very snug within the notch you made. You could also use a bolt or some other repurposed material if you desire.

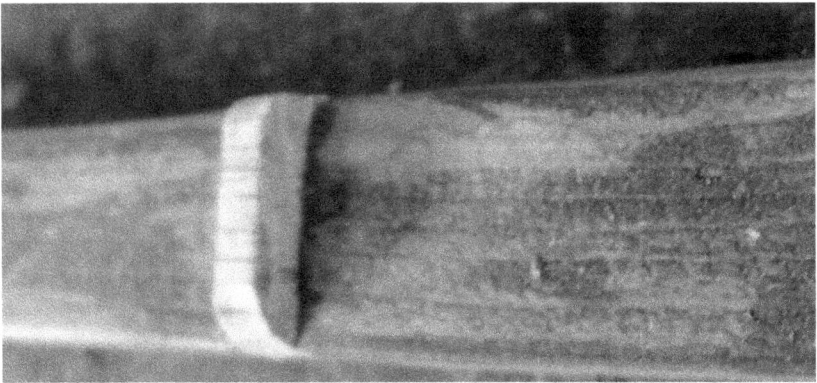

Here is the Nut glued into the notch and slightly rounded. You can now make a small notch in the middle for the string to sit in using a small file or a knife.

Add the peg tuner **(See Page 11-20)** You could easily add a geared tuner such as the ones installed on the Relic 4 String build **(See Page 62)**

Drill a small hole in the opposite end of the neck (the tailpiece) for the string to pass through. Make the hole just big enough for the string.

All that will remain now is to stain or ebonize the finish **(see page 44-47 for ebonizing)** and then add a string to the instrument.

Other options to consider would be drilling a sound hole and/or installing an electric pickup. (**see page 118-122 for adding a pickup**)

Relic Style
Four String Guitar

Once you have mastered the Diddley Bow then you are ready to move on to the three and four string Cigar Box Guitars. The three and four string varieties offer a bit more versatility. The optional fretboards and/or alternate tunings make them an item of interest for even the most seasoned of players. In recent years we have seen Paul McCartney, Johnny Depp, Billy Gibbons, Tom Waits, Steven Tyler, Jack White and many, many other celebrities and musicians sporting cigar box guitars.

This is my most popular guitar and boy have I made my fair share of them.

This is a very traditional, primitive style and it has an incredible tone.

The box used for this example is a modern Davidoff Tubos Special R cigar box. I prefer boxes that are at least 9 inches long. For thin wood or cardboard boxes you will need to add bracing. **See page 148-149**

I use a technique called Ebonizing to distress the wood and give it a sun bleached, dirty, weathered look. **See page 44-47**

Select your wood and then mark off the area for the headstock as well as marking off where to trim. You'll want the neck to be one and one half inches wide. This size is perfect for both three and four string instruments.

Go ahead and leave the headstock square and bulky for now. We will have time to trim and shape it later if desired. Many fine antique examples of these guitars make use of the plain square headstock, however, there are also just as many examples where the builder took a more elegant route and made something much more than functional.

Simple is fine but challenge yourself occasionally.

If using a table saw, cut the left side first, then cut the right side. Use safety precautions including glasses and push boards.

We aren't cutting the entire length of the board because of the headstock area. This is why we cut the left side first. Otherwise the still attached right side would have a cut and a gap and when we cut the left side it would almost certainly cause it to be crooked when we pushed it though.

This is how it should look after the cuts.

Use a fret board the same size as your neck. I either buy them pre cut or cut them using a table saw.

The fretboard should be 1/4 of an inch or so thick.

It is imperative that it lays completely flush on the neck. If not, sand, plane or use another piece of wood.

It will only take a musician a few seconds to know if an instrument was built with quality in mind and the neck is crucial.

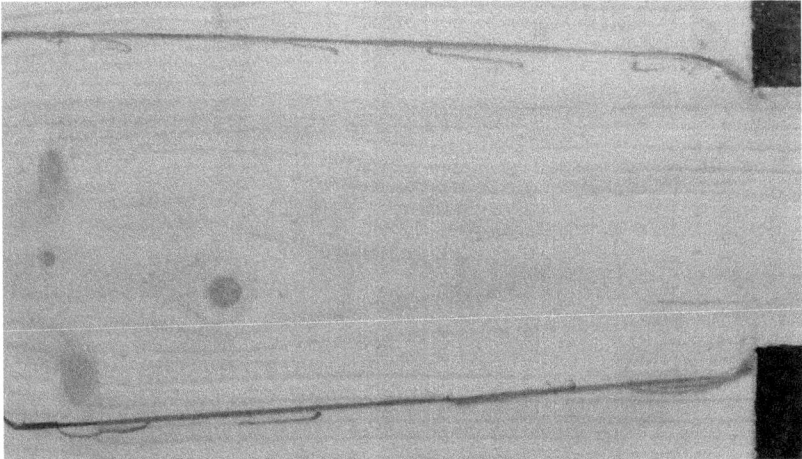

For the headstock lightly outline the shape desired.
Then let the pencil lines get darker and darker as it gets
closer to what you want.

When satisfied, use a band saw or a coping saw to cut
and shape it.

Use sandpaper or a belt sander to true it up and smooth
it out.

Continued on page 48

The Relic look

You can utilize several methods to give an instrument a relic, aged look. Distressing the wood, ebonizing and aging metal parts are simple and very effective methods of reaching this goal.

Distressing the wood

Take a scrap piece of wood and drive four or five small nails through the end. Now you can use this as a sort of a torture hammer for your instrument. I take it and tap it up and down the neck (sometimes the box) to provide a nice aged / wormhole look.

You may want to experiment on a piece of wood that is the same type as your instruments neck. The reason for that is different types of wood may need to be struck harder than others especially if you are going to also ebonize the wood. Ebonizing can cause the wood surface to swell enough to actually remove many nicks, dings and scratches. Softer woods such as pine and poplar will heal more readily than harder wood.

Try not to strike the wood with any noticeable pattern. Rotate the direction of your strikes often.

Remember to strike the edges of the neck.

A regular hammer or even a piece of old pipe can be used to add some more controlled damage to the instrument. I also tap and flatten corners and edges that are commonly damaged on instruments.

Another method I use frequently is to take a small wood screw and drag it in short bursts in various areas. You want to give the look of a worm or some other wood eating insect therefore try not to make the lines too straight. Give it some good zigs and zags, some longer some shorter. Again, don't forget the edges, even consider going over edges or turning corners.

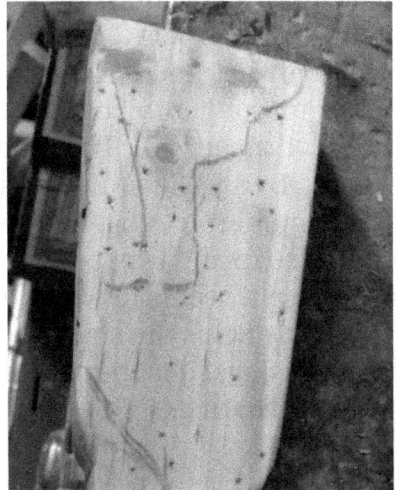

Ebonizing

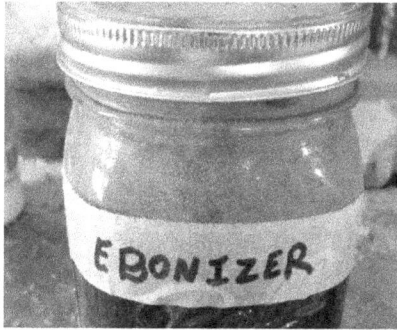

Ebonizing wood is a very effective method of making your wood projects look old. It gives the wood a dry weathered look.

Ebonizing is a chemical process that causes wood to change colors. The tannic acid in the wood determines the darkness of the color. Some woods such as oak will turn almost completely black. Pine will usually turn brown. You'll want to test an area before you do a full application to make sure it's the look you are going for. Be sure and let it dry thoroughly because sometimes it will start out looking jet black and then eventually dry and settle into a mild grayish hue.

I use a mason jar to hold my solution of white vinegar and shredded steel wool. The grade of the steel wool doesn't really matter. By shredded I mean that I use my hands and just pull it in to numerous small pieces. Many people wash their steel wool in soap and warm water to remove protective oils but shredding it seems to work just fine.

Shredding helps the steel wool rust faster. You can also use steel nails, just just be sure and sand them a bit to remove any anti-rust coating.

It typically takes several days before the steel breaks down enough to be effective. It will look clear for quite some time and this in no way reflects if it will work or not. After a month or two you may notice a rusty film collecting on the top of the Vinegar. Some people remove this but I leave it. I typically use a small paint brush to apply the solution and I just push beyond the rusty layer. If you want you can strain out the rusty mess with a paper coffee filter.

Sand the wood before applying. You'll definitely want to wear gloves when applying this because it will stain your skin. Treat it just like any other stain in your workshop.

I keep one jar of white vinegar and steel wool and another jar with the same solution but diluted with water. I use the later mostly on hard woods where I want the effect to be more subtle.

I prefer using both ebonizing and stain to achieve a relic look. First, take a cotton swab or small paint brush and place it sparingly in various places of the wood. Once that dries, wipe it down well with a cotton cloth and then apply a stain with a reddish hue. I like red mahogany the best. These two together make a really nice weathered patina.

To age metal parts:
Ammonia, while terrible to breathe, is a great way to age brass parts. Place the brass in a zip lock bag and add a couple of ammonia soaked cotton balls and wait a day or two and you will have some nice patina on them. Other metal parts will need to be rubbed with steel wool or fine sandpaper first and you may want to also add some salt to the mix.

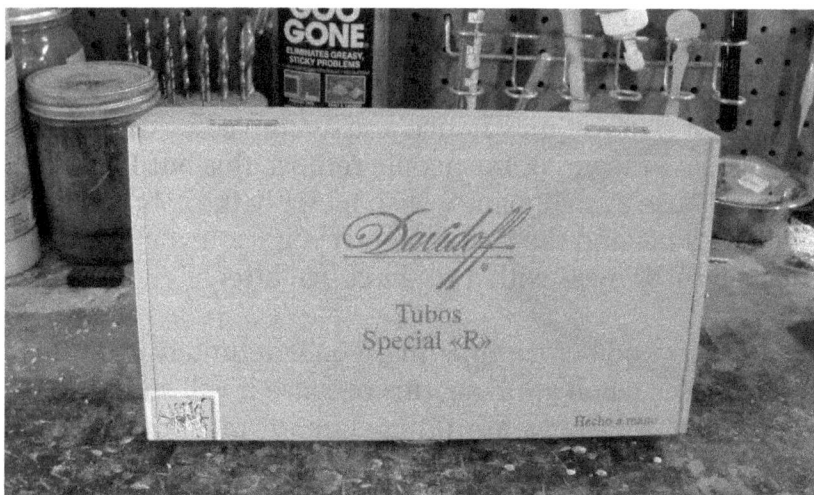

Before Ebonizing

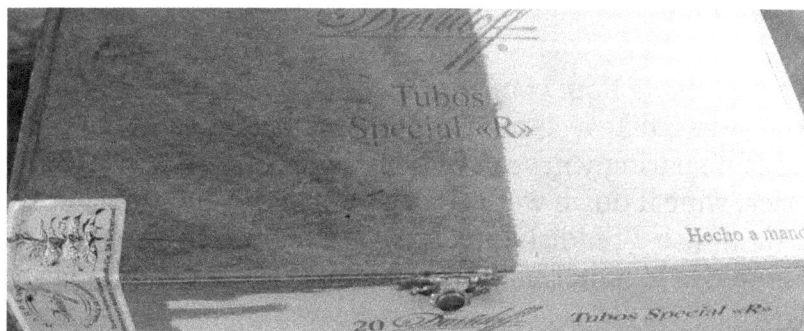

Here we see the effect of Ebonizing.
Different woods react differently to Ebonizing so it's
advised that you test a small section and let it dry
completely before you continue.

I normally test an area inside of the box first.

After you have applied your finish, whether it is ebonizing or stain or both, consider other ways to give your instrument an attic or barn find look to it.

Running your thumb across a paintbrush to flick small specks of paint works well too.

A good water stain here or there can also be a nice touch.

Don't be afraid to rub some good old fashioned dirt on it if necessary.

continued from page 41

Lay the neck on the box, make sure it is centered and square then mark each side.

Use a square to mark out the area that needs to be cut. The depth should equal the height of the neck.

You are striving for a snug fit all around. Use a hand saw to make the side cuts. Account for the thickness of your blade. The bottom cut is best made with an exacto knife by scoring it many times then popping it out. The exacto is also helpful in shaving it out if it is too tight initially.

It's always better to cut too little than too much.
Take your time.

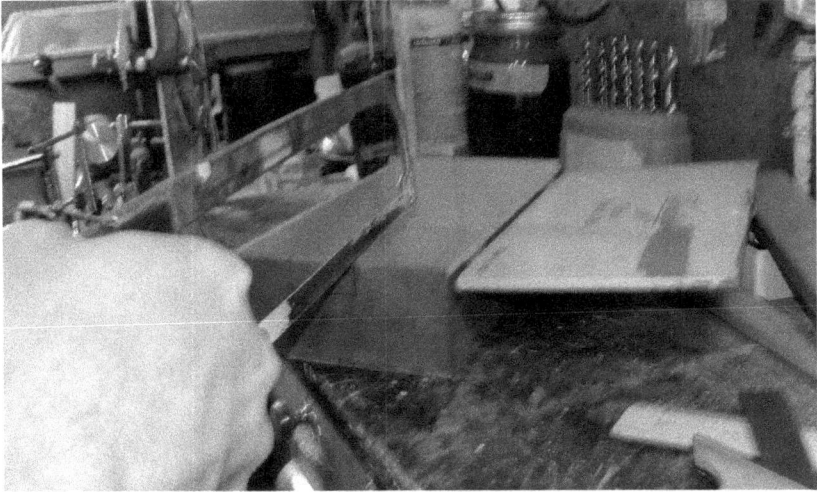

Hand saw the edge cuts.

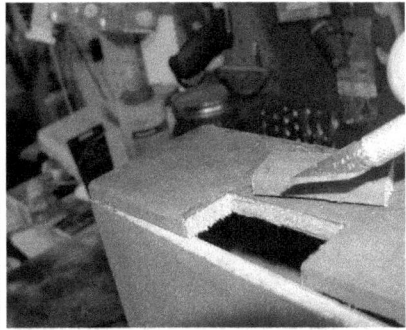

Use the exacto knife to score the bottom.

This works well on most boxes but you can also use the cutting wheel attachment on a dremel.

Regardless of method, make the cuts straight and make sure the neck fit is snug.

Fit the neck into the box.

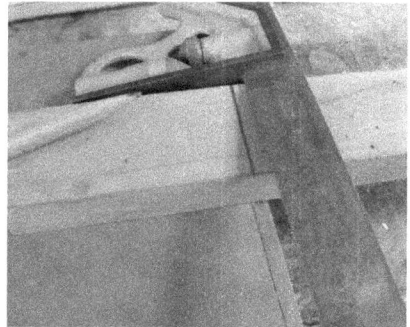

The neck should be trimmed down so that the fretboard will sit level with the box lid once it is glued into place.

Determine where the neck should be trimmed and use your square to mark it off.

The goal is to trim it down to accommodate the height of the lid. We will be attaching a fret board to this instrument later and we need everything to lay nice and flat.

Use a table saw, band saw or hand saw to trim.

The finished cut after using the table saw with the blade raised to the height of the cigar box lid.

Place the neck back in the box and test the fit.

A perfect fit. The neck is completely level with the lid.

Next, cut pieces of wood that will sit inside of the box and provide a surface to mount the neck to.

The box here required two pieces of oak that were cut to the exact width of the box. Trimming (with the table saw) the height of one of the boards so that the neck would sit at exactly the right height.

Use wood glue to install the blocks of wood.

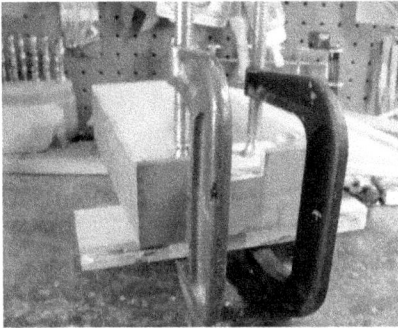

Clamp into place and allow them to dry completely.

Wipe away any excess glue.

Use a scrap piece of wood under the box so that my clamp doesn't damage the wood.

Make sure the neck is square
then drill holes for the wood
screws that will hold it in place.

Countersink the holes just enough for them to not touch
the lid. A generous amount of wood glue is applied before
installing the screws and washers. They only need to be
snug, do not over tighten.

While the glue is drying in the previous step, move on to the fretboard.

This example uses a separate fretboard about 1/4 of an inch thick that will be glued on to the neck later in the build. Even though it is a separate fretboard, the method of fretting is the same as that shown on **pages 85-102**

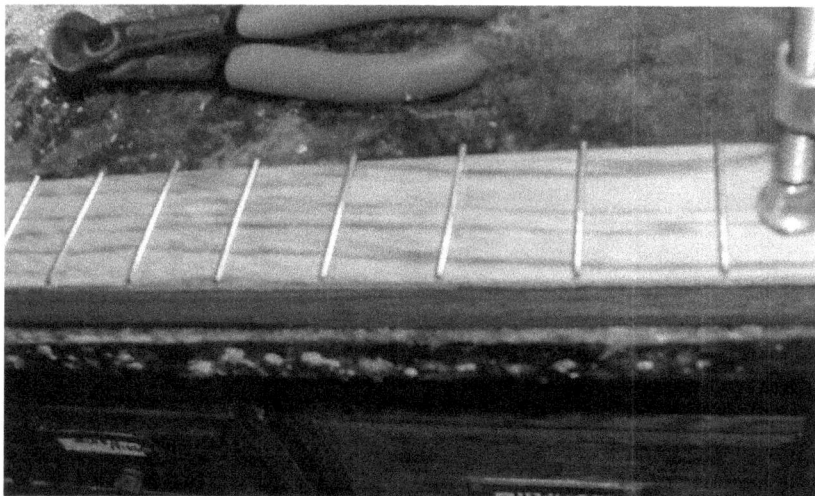

Once the board is fretted and filed, add the fret position markers (**see page 77-78**)

Once this is done set it aside and move on to the tailpiece.

Above is what the completed Tailpiece will look like from the front and the rear.

First, make sure the grain is in the proper direction. Mount it so that the grain is running up and down. The reason for this is because the tension of the strings, which will be in a straight line, can easily cause the wood to break on a grain line. I recommend you use a hardwood for the tailpiece.

I keep a concert ukulele Nut in my shop and use it as a template for where my string holes will be drilled.

Use pop rivet casings as string ferrules.

Drill the string holes with a drill bit one size smaller than the pop rivet casing. Then drill about half the length of the rivet with a drill bit of equal size. This allows the rivet to be lightly tapped in where they will be held firmly in place. Use a bit of wood glue if necessary.

Hold the rivet lightly using pliers. Then tap the rivet pin onto your workbench or a scrap piece of wood and it will easily separate.

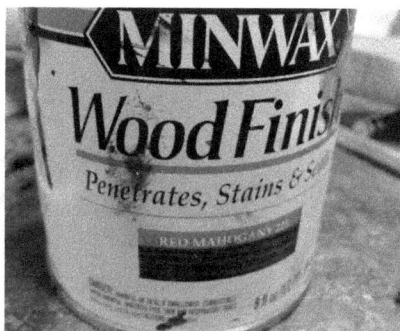

Age / distress the tailpiece (**see page 43-48**) using a combination of ebonizing and staining. I apply ebonizing solution with a cotton swab to a few areas and then apply the stain.

Notice the direction of wood grain in relation to where the string holes are drilled.

Attach the tailpiece to the box. Measure carefully to ensure that you remain lined up with the neck. Add a support block inside of the box for the bridge to attach to as well as the lid to rest against which will help support the bridge.

Drill the soundhole

This could be done at almost any point during the build. I prefer to wait until after I have installed the internal support for the neck. This way I know where I can cut to prevent the wood I added from showing. Remember to leave room for the bridge.

Hole cutters come in a variety of sizes.
It is recommended that you use a drill press if possible.

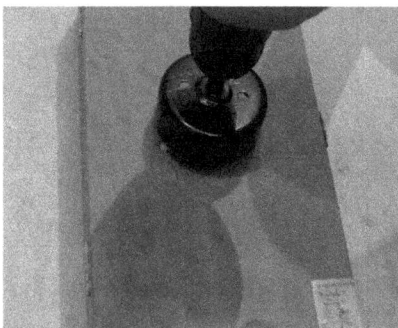

Be sure to line up the hole with the placement of the neck.

A scrap piece of wood inside the box prevents damaging the bottom of the box.

Install the Piezo Pickup and the 1/4 Jack

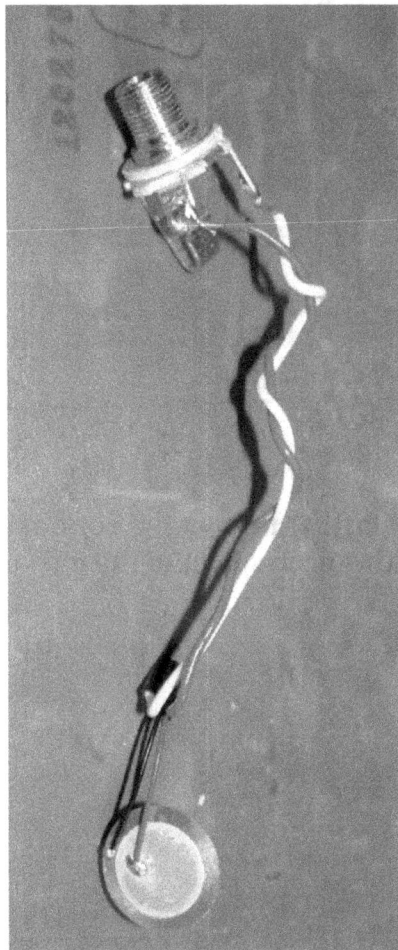

Piezo soldered and ready to be mounted.

Cut wire to be only slightly longer than what's needed.

I keep a tiny micro amp in my shop so I can test the pickups and wiring before I close everything up.

Install the Tuners

Use a drillpress to make the holes for the tuners.
Mark where you want your tuners to sit. Make sure they are even on both sides.

Place the top two tuners slightly farther in than the bottom two. This allows the strings to flow nicely down to the nut.

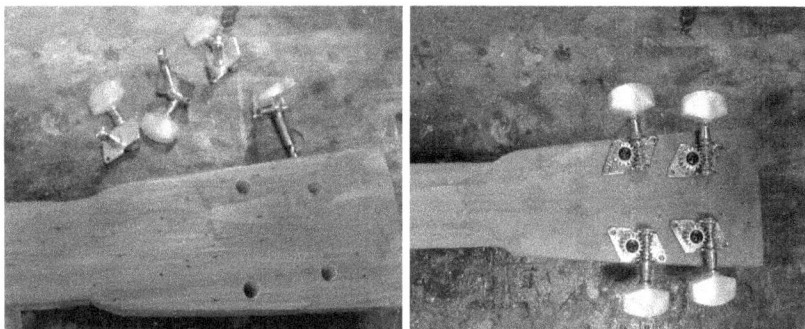

Drill slowly to prevent the wood from splintering when the bit pops through.

It's best to drill so that the drill bit pops out on the side that the tuner is mounted on. This way any splintering is covered by the tuner itself.

Make the Bridge

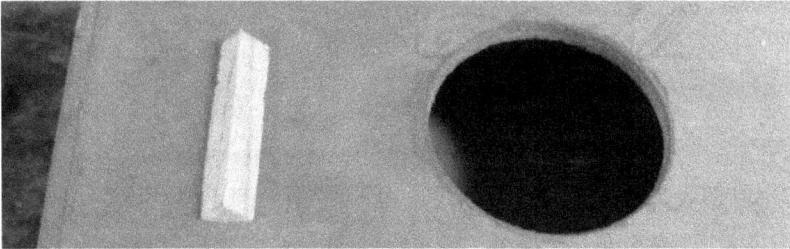

With this being a Relic build, use an old school type of bridge. Use the band saw and carefully cut a pyramid shaped bridge out of a piece of oak or similar hardwood. It's important that the strings have only a small area of contact. This prevents buzzing and provides a fuller sound. The height is important. You want the strings to be level as they run down the neck. Sand or shim if necessary or simply cut a new piece if the height is off. This is a floating bridge meaning it is not glued or tacked down. This allows it to be moved/adjusted for proper intonation. In theory the bridge should be the same distance from the 12th fret that the nut and the 12th fret are. You want to make sure that you have a perfect harmonic at the 12th fret. String height, string gauge, tuning tension, these can all have an impact on the intonation and a floating bridge provides the freedom to make slight adjustments whenever necessary. With that said, a great deal of guitarists slide it to where it's really close and then just tack it down. Even Brian Setzer with his vintage 1959 Gretsch used double-sided carpet tape to hold his floating bridge in place.

See page 171-176 for more bridge options.

With everything now ready for the fretboard to be attached, lightly sand the top of the neck and back of the fretboard.

Apply wood glue to the neck and then lay the fretboard in place. Make sure everything is lined up properly.
Lay another piece of wood on top of the fretboard and then starting in the middle work you way out to each end, attaching clamps to hold the fretboard down. Wipe away excess glue as it squeezes out of the edges. I crowd as many clamps on the neck as I possibly can.
Alternating clamps from one side to the other helps prvent the fretboard from drifting out of place.

Let the wood glue dry for several hours before you remove the clamps.

I used a ukulele Nut for this instrument but you could use a bolt or bone or even hard wood for the nut. Just make sure the height of your nut and bridge are comparable. String height should be a bit higher for slide guitar playing. Otherwise keep the action fairly low but not so low as to cause buzzing. When the string is too high you will actually change the pitch of the string as you fret it. This will be especially noticeable on the first 2 or 3 frets. Carefully file the string notches lower if necessary. For a Nut that is too low you could pry it loose and add some wood filler. Once that is dry sand it flat and then glue the nut back on.

Seen page 123-126 for adding a string retainer.

The completed Relic 4 String.

Tenor Hubcap Banjo

From a Folk Art perspective I felt I would be remiss if I didn't show a method of building an nice stringed instrument with something other than the already beloved cigar box.

The possibilities are quite endless. Boat oars, wooden ironing boards, motorcycle gas tanks, oil cans... Clearly the list goes on and on. I have seen and built examples of all of these.

But the hubcap banjo, well, people just absolutely love these. They definitely have a cool factor and it's no doubt an awesome conversation piece and oh yes you can play some really great music on it too.

Keep in mind that I am only showing one method of making a hubcap banjo. You could easily flip the hubcap over and stretch a piece of hide across the opening and be more in alignment with a traditional banjo. Perhaps cut out a piece of plywood to use as the soundboard. I think you can see that the sky is the limit.

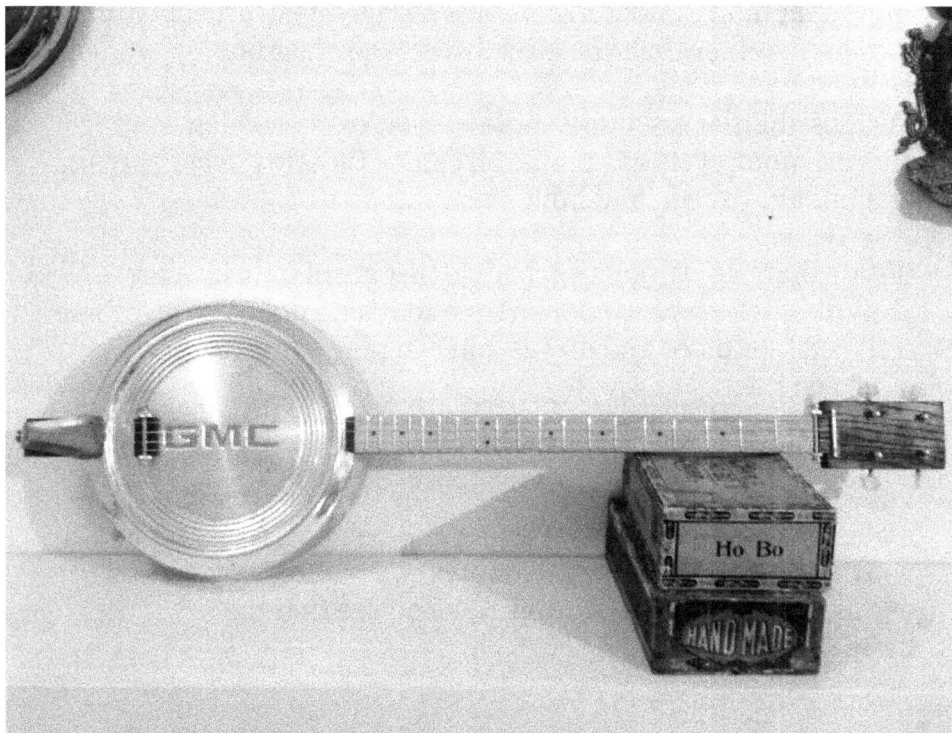

Here she is, the 4 string tenor hubcap banjo. Brass bolt for the Nut, brass string retainer, oak and brass bolt for the bridge and an old, steel, shoe horn that I used for the tailpiece.

There are a few things to keep in mind when picking out the perfect hubcap. I am fond of hubcaps made in the 60's and 70's but there are many others that will work just as well.

I prefer for them to be at least 2 inches deep but I'm flexible on that too.

The primary thing I look for is one that has very little rise or hump on top. The higher the hump, the higher the neck has to be to prevent the strings from touching before they reach the bridge.

For the neck I used a large piece of oak. Using the table saw I cut strips from each side so that my fretboard would be an inch and a half wide. I left the headstock wider which gives the freedom to shape it later or leave it the way it is to give an old school paddle board look.

The length of this board will be determined by several factors: the scale length desired, the size of the hubcap and the placement of the bridge.

Make sure that the board you use is completely flat and contains no twists. Use a sander or plane if necessary.

When choosing wood I will use a long metal ruler and lay the edge against the board and look for any rise, drop or twist. If the board looks like it will be more trouble than its worth then I will, more often than not, use it for something other than the neck.

The neck is, in my opinion, the most important component. It is where you will spend the majority of your build time (assuming you choose to fret the instrument).

Use a fret template to determine where the bridge will sit. **See page 93-95** for more about fret templates.

Place the hubcap on the neck to see exactly where the bridge should go.

The line and arrow on my fret template indicates bridge placement.

With the placement determined you can mark where the neck can be cut off. The cut is made exactly where the neck touches the hubcap. We will cut another piece later that will run completely through the hub cap where the neck will attach.

I use the table saw to make the cut but this can also be done with the bandsaw or hand saw.

Mark where the Nut will go.
For this instrument I will be fretting the neck directly.
See page 85-102 for more about fretting.

Make a couple of cuts with the fret saw for the nut and use a small screwdriver or chisel to pop out the wood.

Cut to the same depth as the fretwire.

Level it with a small file or sandpaper.

Round of the bottom edges of the neck

Flip the neck over and mark off about 1/4 inch on each side from the headstock to approximately the 12th fret area.

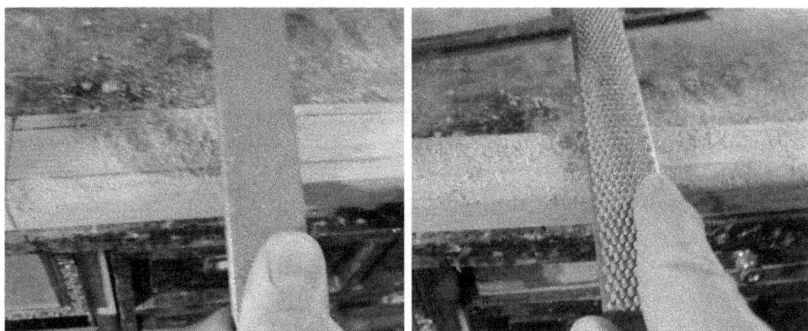

Clamp the neck down. Using a rasp, round off and shape the neck within the area marked.

Finish by using the flat side of the rasp followed by sandpaper.

Rounding off the back edges of the neck makes playing the instrument so much more enjoyable.

Fret Position Markers

Fret position markers are typically made using either mother of pearl, abalone, plastic or clay inlays.

A much simpler and more rustic method is to use a wood burner to place the marks on frets 3, 5, 7, 9, 12, 15, 17 and 19.

Position inlays are fairly inexpensive and are quite easy to install. If you choose to go this route I would advise you to acquire Forstner bits or Brad Point drill bits. Using a drill press is the best way to control the depth. You can add a drop of super glue or wood glue before you press them in.
Get them as close to flush as possible. Most materials can be sanded lightly to make them flush.

Fancier inlays with custom designs will require a router and some good quality downcut inlay router bits.

Cutting your own inlays is another way to take your builds to the next level. You'll need a jewelers saw to cut the mother of pearl or abalone. A word of caution though, please use a breathing mask when cutting this material.

The dust is in no way good for your lungs. There are numerous books related to inlaying and engraving so I am not going to go into any great detail here. Stewart MacDonald sells a pearl cutting set that comes with a saw, cutting jig, air pump, cutting lubricant and a scribe as well as a book that is very beneficial, the entire set is less than one hundred dollars.

You can also use any number of other materials for your inlays. Just make sure they are flush with the fretboard. I've used copper tacks on occasion. For those you need to pre-drill and countersink.

Mother of Pearl Inlay Position Markers

Wood burned Position Markers

When woodburning the inlays, set the burner to its highest setting and burn for 8 to 10 seconds on hardwoods.

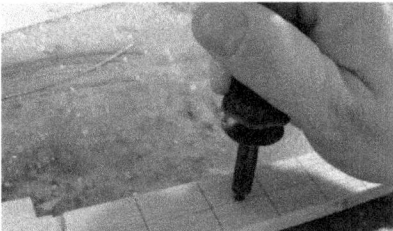

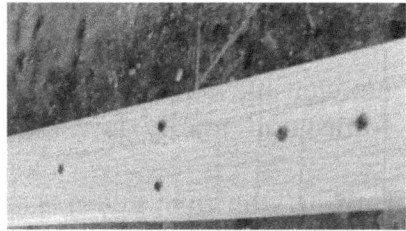

Draw a line straight down the neck and mark where you want the position markers.

On Fret 12 I use 2 markers which is very common. This indicates the octave change.

Cut out the openings for the neck support/heel board.

Lay a piece of wood the same size as your neck on the hubcap and using a pencil, mark on the hubcap where it will enter and exit. You want to make sure it is in the center.

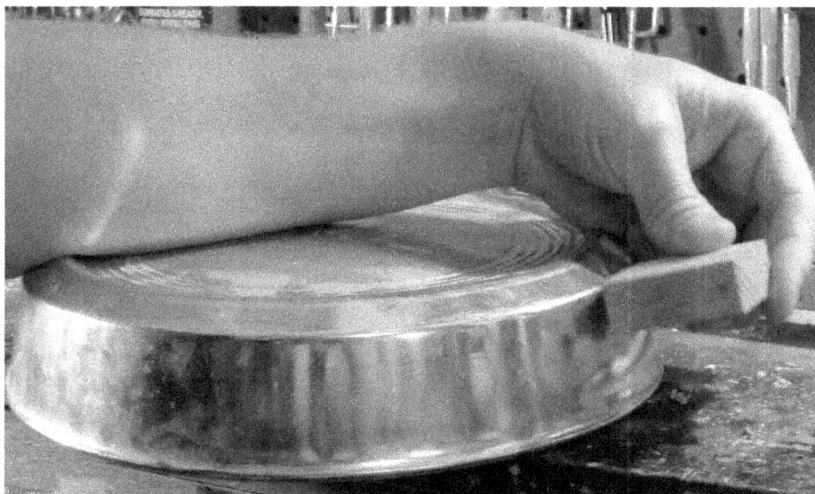

Use a piece of wood the same width and height as the neck and mark where the cuts will be made.

Dremel with cutting wheel attachment.

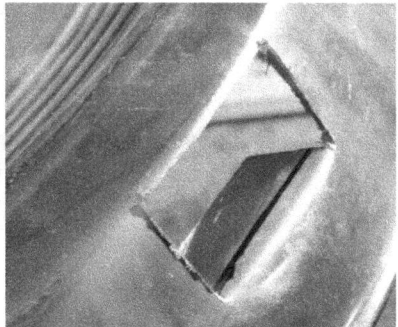

Always use safety glasses!
The dremel can throw shards at unbelievably high speeds.

Some hubcaps will create lots of sparks so be careful around anything flammable. A workshop covered in sawdust is not advisable.

It is imperative to **cut only three sides.** The folded metal flap will be used later to attach the neck.

81

Run a board the same width as the neck through the hubcap. Leave enough room for the tailpiece on the end. Sit the neck on top of this board and mark the bottom. This will in essence be the heel of the guitar. It should extend to approx. the 12th fret (where you stopped using the rasp earlier.

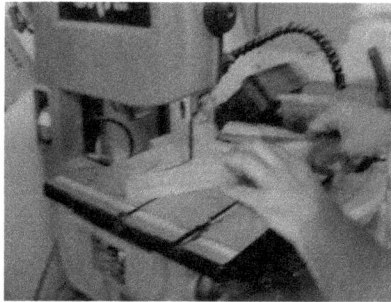

The heel needs to taper to allow a musicians hand access to the bottom frets. The photo on the next page shows what the finished cut should look like.

Use a band saw or hand saw to cut.

Sand thoroughly. Make sure this piece is smooth and level.
The neck will be glued and bolted onto this piece later.

Inside view of the hubcap.

The metal cut earlier is folded down so that you can drill a hole later and use wood screws to hold it in place.

Fretting the Neck

Fretting

There is a great joy when starting out building roots instruments. Even more in using nothing but found or repurposed parts. These are typically of the fretless variety. There does seem to come a time when the builder wants to express yet another degree of craftsmanship. Fretting is a logical next step.

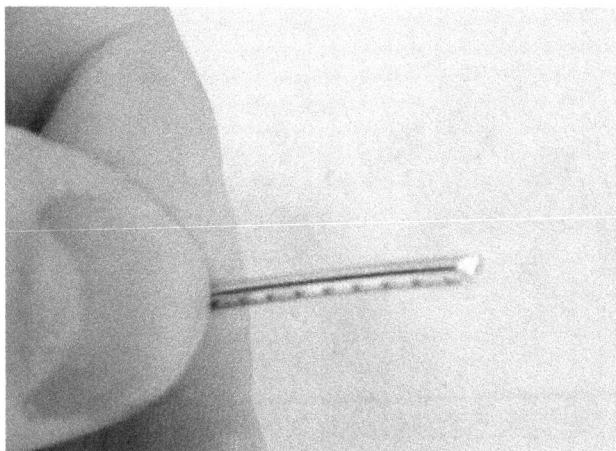

Fretwire has a crown which is the fatter top portion of the wire and the tang which is the lower skinny portion.

The tang usually has little jagged teeth that assist in holding the fretwire down inside the fretboard.

Fretwire size is based on the width and the height of the crown as well as the height of the tang.

It is important that when you saw the fret slots that you cut to the depth of the tang. If you undercut the slot then the fret will not seat properly.

The saw that I recommend is an adjustable Fret slotting saw with a depth stop. It allows you to set the depth to the tang height of whatever fret wire you use.

I purchased mine from **http://stewmac.com**

You can also buy a fret blade for table saws. There are all sorts of devices and jigs designed to assist with cutting frets.

I like doing work as primitively as possible but I would not skimp on a fretting saw.

The purpose of a fret is to divide the neck into intervals. When using a standard musical scale, each fret is considered one semitone and 12 semitone's equals one octave. For example, the top E string of an acoustic guitar fretted once becomes an F, 2nd fret is F#, 3rd fret G and so on. Once you reach the 12th fret it becomes E again but of the next octave.

Many builders use Dulcimer fretting which uses the diatonic scale. This is an 8 note scale with 7 pitches and then the repeating octave.

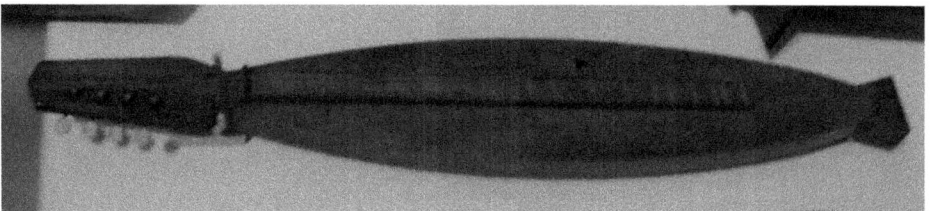

Dulcimer

The scale length is the distance from the Nut to the bridge.

For proper intonation, the distance from the Nut to the 12th fret is the same as the distance from the 12th fret to the bridge. For example, with a 25 inch scale the distance from the Nut to the 12th fret would be 12.5 inches and the 12th fret to the bridge would also be 12.5 inches.

There are several ways to determine the fret spacing. One method is to know the math and/or use a fret calculator. **http://www.stewmac.com/FretCalculator**

There are many of these available on line that tell you precisely the distance of each fret from the Nut for whatever scale length you wish to use.

When I first started fretting guitars I took a guitar I owned that had a 25 1/2 scale and by using a narrow piece of wood I marked the position of each fret and then used this as my template.

Later I purchased a cardboard fret template from C. B. Gitty (**cbgitty.com**) that showed various scale lengths. I highly recommend this. I also own a metal fret template with a 25 inch scale which is the most common scale length that I use.

Throughout this book I will be using a wood template with a 25 inch scale.

The wood I used for the template is a piece of pine off of a typical yard sale sign that you can obtain at nearly any hardware store.

See page 93-95 for more on fret templates

I frequently use medium fretwire but I also really like using high fretwire. High fretwire makes note bending easier and requires less pressure to produce a clean tone and it essentially serves the same purpose as scalloped (carved out) frets which so many speed players prefer.

The tools I will be using: fret template, clamps, fretwire cutters, hammer, small block of wood and a dremel with sanding wheel attachment.

You can choose to fret the neck itself or you can fret a separate board that you attach to the neck. On the next page is an example of a separate fretboard.

You can buy or cut your fretboard's using a variety of woods. They are typically about 1/4 of an inch thick. The most popular woods are rosewood and maple, zebra wood and oak works nicely as well.

I highly recommend you use a separate fretboard when your neck is not a hardwood. The fretboard will add a great deal of strength and stability. I have used pine and poplar necks with hardwood fretboards with great success.

Some builders add a bit of super glue or wood glue to their fretwire. There are many debates for and against this practice.

When I first started fretting, my cuts weren't quite perfect and so I used wood glue. I would take a scrap piece of wood and squeeze out some glue upon it and then I would drag the tang of my fretwire through it before hammering it in. You should immediately wipe any glue off of the fretboard especially if you plan to stain it later.

Above is an example of a separate fretboard. I use this when I build the Relic 4 string Cigar box guitar. Once fretted it is glued and clamped into place on the neck.

I occasionally purchase wood for my fretboards from
rockler.com
The harware store typically carries nice selections of oak and poplar and occassionally some slightly nicer varities.

Fret Templates

Using a straight piece of wood that was approximately 35 inches long, I created a Fret template that I lay on my boxes so I can see where the final frets will be as well as the bridge. Note the arrow and line to the left of the clamp indicating the bridge position. This template uses the 25 inch scale which is the one I use most often. This quickly allows me to see where any sound hole will be drilled, where the fretboard will lay and how much room I have for a tailpiece.

It's best to know up front where everything will be so you can understand all of your options.

A steel Fret template purchased from StewMac.com

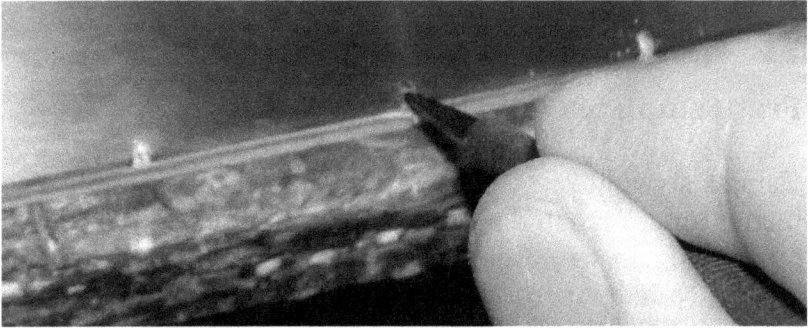

Using its notches you can quickly mark the edge of your fretboard. They come with two scale length's, one on each side.

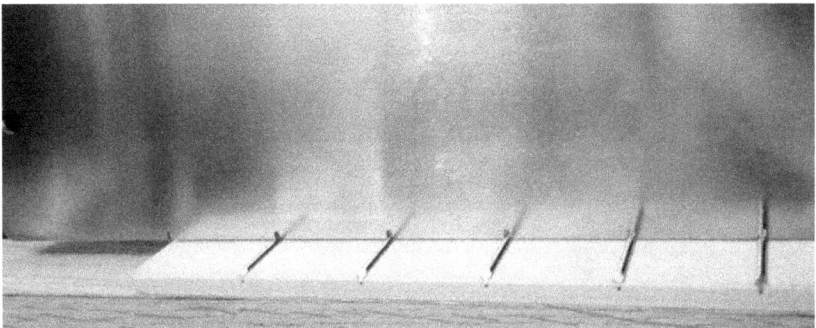

It is also a great way to see if your fretboard is level.

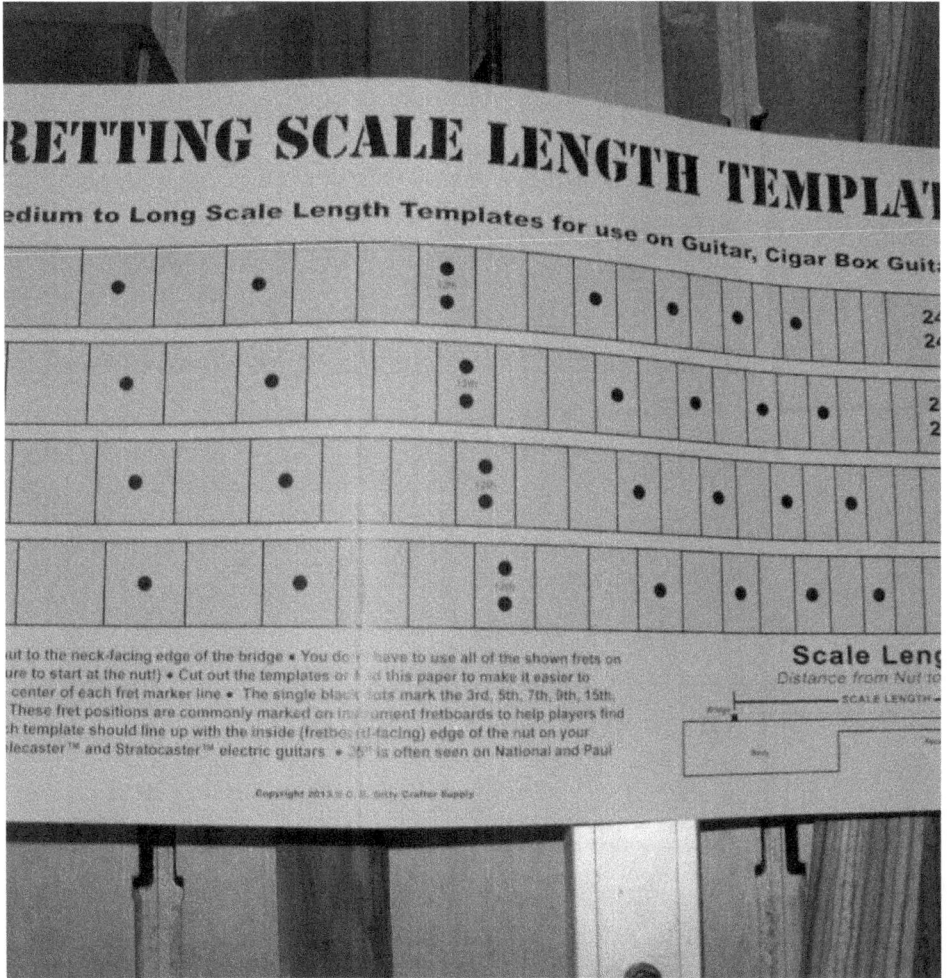

RETTING SCALE LENGTH TEMPLA

edium to Long Scale Length Templates for use on Guitar, Cigar Box Guit

ut to the neck-facing edge of the bridge • You do n' have to use all of the shown frets on
ure to start at the nut!) • Cut out the templates of t d this paper to make it easier to
center of each fret marker line • The single blac' ots mark the 3rd, 5th, 7th, 9th, 15th,
These fret positions are commonly marked on ins ument fretboards to help players find
h template should line up with the inside (fretbo 'd-facing) edge of the nut on your
lecaster™ and Stratocaster™ electric guitars • 6" is often seen on National and Paul

Copyright 2013 © C. B. Gitty Crafter Supply

Scale Leng

Distance from Nut to

This is a good cardboard fretting template with various scale length's available from **cbgitty.com**

Using a fret template or fret calculator, mark where the nut and frets will be.

Stand the fret template on its edge and make a tiny mark on the neck for each fret.

Next use a square to draw each fret line.

Clamp the neck to prevent it from moving around.

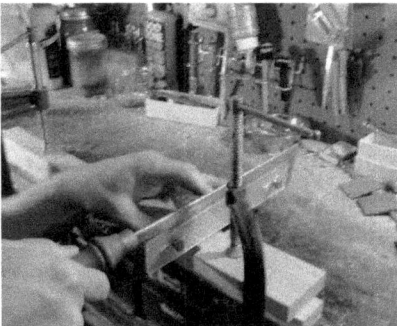

Adjust the fret saw to the depth of the fretwire's tang. Use one hand to steady the saw then do a couple of slow back pulls before sawing back and forth.

Sand lightly after all of the cuts have been made.

Using the back side of an exacto helps clean the fret cuts out after the sanding. Any debris left behind can cause the fret to not seat properly.

Make sure the edges of the neck are slightly rounded to prevent splintering.

Begin by clamping the neck down. My work bench is chest high which allows me to work without bending over. I clamp the neck to the edge of the bench to allow proper access. When necessary I unclamp the neck and turn it to the opposite direction. For example when it's time to file each side of the frets.

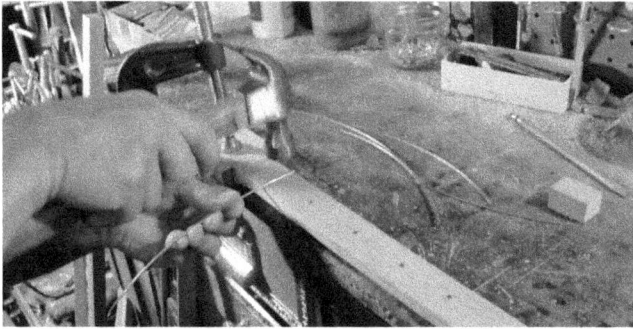

The proper tool would be a brass fretting hammer.
I carefully, and lightly, tap the fretwire into the slot with a regular hammer, striking as flat as possible.

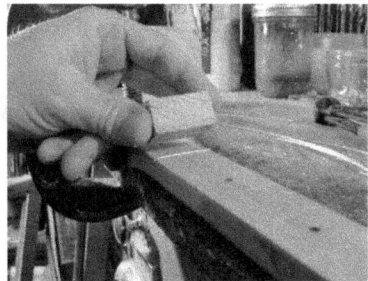

Once the wire is in place, use fretwire cutters to clip of the excess.

Use a scrap piece of hardwood and a clamp to press the fret into the wood.

It's a bit tedious, but pressing the frets individually ensures they are seated to the proper depth and that they are flat.

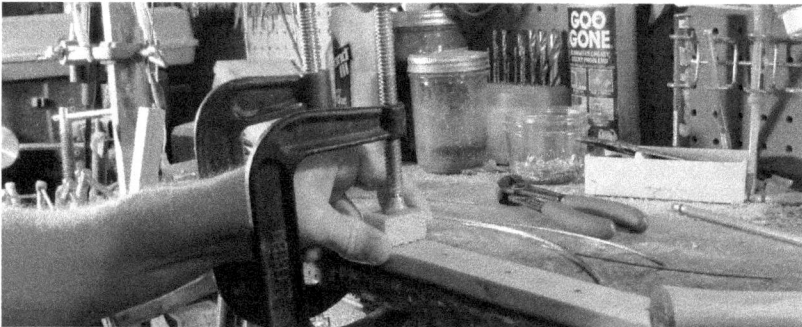

Hammer, cut, press, hammer, cut, press hammer, cut, press... Lay a metal ruler on its edge upon the frets to see if any are too high. High frets will cause a buzz or a dead fret. A high fret may need to be pressed again or filed down.

Dressing the Frets

Once all of the frets are in place and pressed level, file the edges. An actual fret file is the preferred method but I use a dremel with a medium coarse wheel. This takes practice and proper precautions.

Regardless of the filing method, it is important that each fret taper off and that there are no sharp edges on the side of the fretboard.

Slowly run a cotton cloth down the edge to see if it catches. If not, then slowly run your fingers down it. Be careful, fret wire can be extremely sharp.

Wear safety glasses! The dremel is a very high speed tool. Protect your eyes.

The finished fret.

Once the neck is fully fretted, leveled and filed, you are then ready to stain it if desired or move on to the next step of the build.

Tuning Keys & The Nut

These are open geared tuners. The gears should point towards the base of the neck.

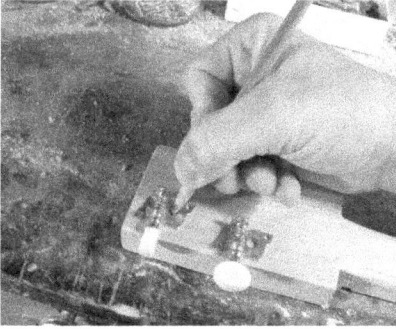

Disassemble the tuners, line them up to where you want them to be and use the holes to mark their position.

Use a square to ensure that the tuners on the opposing side are perfectly aligned. I like for my top two tuners to sit a bit further in than the two below. This allows the stings to flow nicely to the Nut.

Marked for proper alignment.

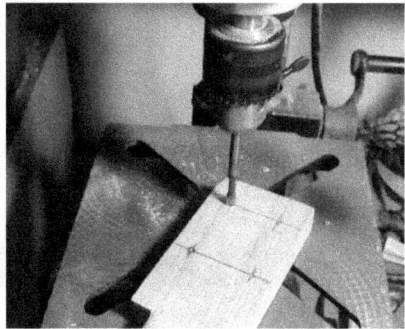

Use a forstner bit that is the same size as the tuner.
The forstner bit helps reduce the chance of splintering the wood.

Use a scrap piece of wood to test the fit.

A drill press will make the holes precise.

After the drilling.

After you stain the wood, attach the tuners which will be held in place with tiny screws. I recommend drilling with a drill bit slightly smaller than the screw before you attach them.

These screws are prone to break especially when you are using hardwood.

If the head should break off you can try using vice grips to grab on and spin the screw back out.

The nut for this instrument is a brass 8-32 bolt.

When using a separate fretboard you may need to go up to 10-32 bolt.

There are times when a larger or smaller bolt is needed. You can also use a file or dremel to flatten the side that sits against the neck.

Here is the bolt in place with knurled brass nuts on each side.

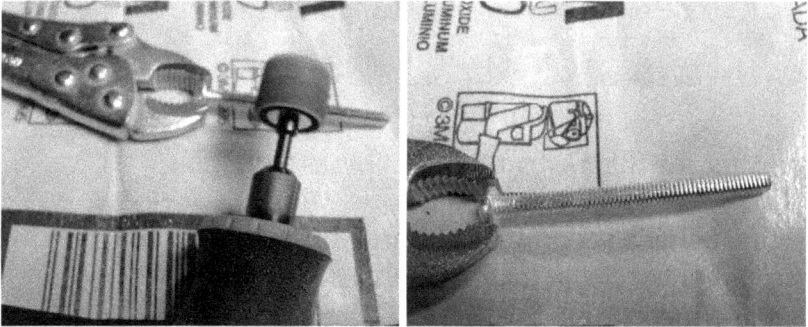

This is an example of filing the bolt to make it the desired height. Use pliers to hold the bolt because it will get exceedingly hot.

Staining the neck

This staining method can be utilized when you have fretted the neck directly and not used a separate fretboard.

First, using masking tape, cover the fretboard and overlap the neck by about 1/4 of an inch or less. Just enough for it to give the appearance of two pieces.

I like leaving the fretboard natural. Sometimes, after I have stained the neck, I will use wood oil on the fretboard to give it a hint of color along with helping the wood from drying out.

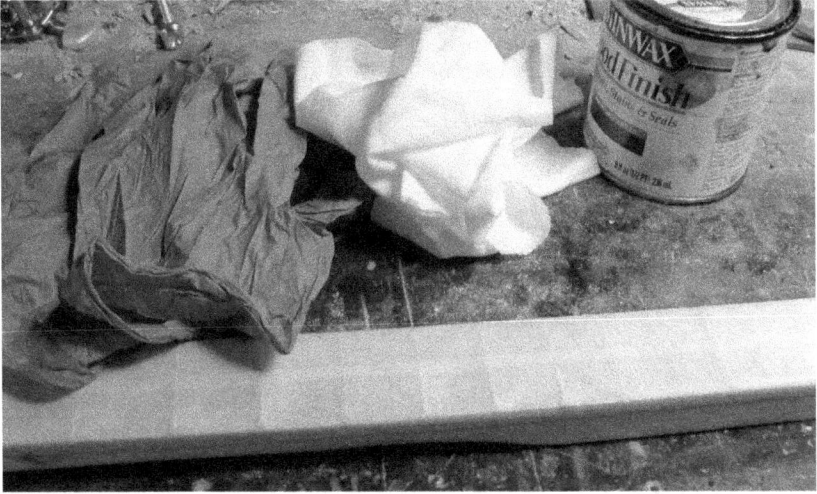

Taped off and ready for staining. Run your fingers along the edges of the tape to make sure it is secure. It's much easier to prevent the stain from going where you don't want it now than to try and remove it later.

Wear gloves when staining. For this build I am using MINWAX Red Mahogany stain, rubbing it into the wood with a piece of cotton cloth.

Rub in the direction of the grain and let it sit for about 5 minutes. Then, use a clean cloth to rub it down and let it dry. Repeat a time or two if you want it darker.

Don't let the stain dry completely on the wood before you wipe it down or it will become gummy.

Here are both parts of the neck, stained, rubbed and drying.

Once dry you can remove the tape. Excess stain can be scrapped off with a razor blade, exacto knife or carefully sanded.

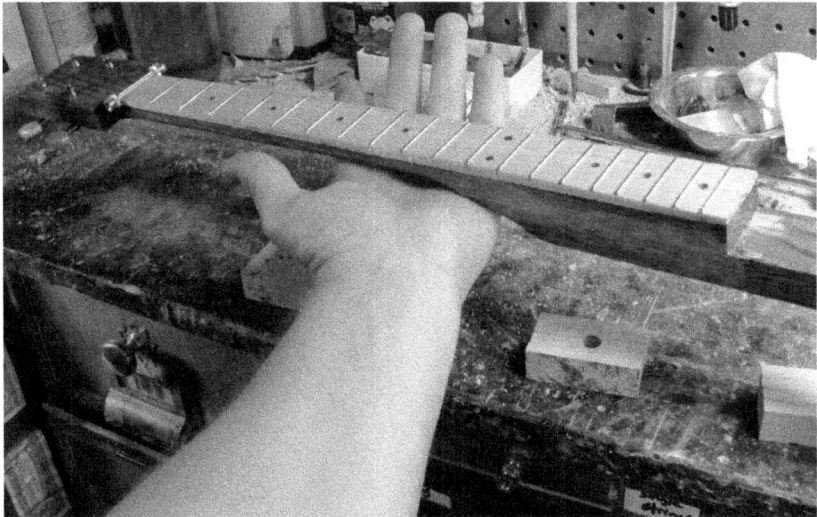

Attach the Neck

First, slide the heel part of the neck into the hubcap making sure it is lined up properly for the tailpiece and the now fretted neck. Use a fret template to make sure everything is in the right place.

Next, turn the hubcap over, place the neck in place and clamp it down. Drill 2 or 3 holes for wood screws. **Making sure not to drill all the way through.**

Also, make sure the wood screws you use are a length that won't go all the way though the neck when you countersink them.

Use a Forstner bit that matches the head of your screw and drill just enough to countersink the screw.

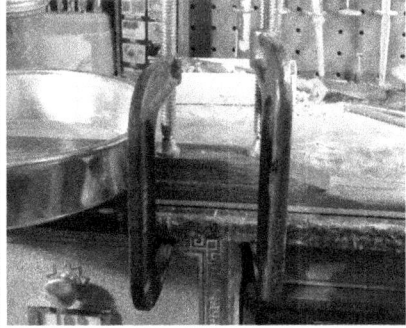

Now undo the clamp and apply wood glue.

Position the neck back in place and reclamp lightly.

Put the wood screws in just enough to know that they are back in the holes you drilled.

Tighten the clamps and then put the screws in completely.

Use wood filler to fill in the holes.

Let the filler dry completely and then sand lightly.

You can touch up the holes with the same color stain you used earlier.

Adding the Jack
&
Piezo Pickup

I spent many frustrating moments with a soldering pencil before I broke down and invested in a good Soldering gun.

You will also need some wire strippers and/or an exacto knife.

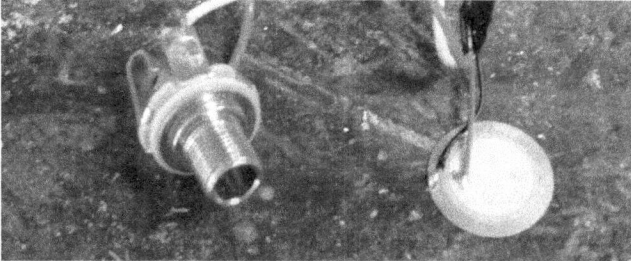

I prefer Piezo's that already have wires soldered to them. I cut some extra wire to the length I need and solder this to the 1/4 inch mono jack and then solder these to the wires of the Piezo. Use an exacto to remove enough insulation from the Piezo's wire. It is usually extremely thin wire and regular wire strippers won't do the trick.

If you buy Piezo's that have no wire attached, simply solder a wire to the brass part of the disk and one wire to the white center of the disk. Just don't let the solder on the brass touch the white part of the disk.

Many times I will mount the Piezo directly to the lid or hubcap just under the bridge. This hubcap is not very strong so I will place a block wedge between the neck and the hubcap. First, cut the wedge so that it fits snug. Next, use a Forstner bit that is the size of the Piezo and drill out enough space for the Piezo to fit into it. Use a chisel or file to notch out a section for the wires to pass through.

Next put some gorilla glue under the piezo and cover this with some masking tape.

The gorilla glue expands as it dries so it will make everything hold very securely once in place.

The hole for the jack:
It can be very challenging to drill a hole into a curved metal surface, to overcome this clamp on a scrap piece of wood and then drill. It holds the bit and prevents it from wandering.

Here is the completed installation of the jack and the pickup.

String Retainer

The neck on this instrument does not have a scarf joint at the headstock. It is completely straight.

This means that the height of the strings at the tuners will be roughly the same height or higher than the Nut.

Without sufficient tension on the Nut the strings will move around or possibly not even sit on the Nut at all.

To compensate for this we install a string retainer.

See page 164-169 for more about a scarf joint

The retainer will be made using 1/8 inch square tubing and #2 x 1/2 inch wood screws. The square tubing comes in both aluminum and brass.

Lay the square tube across the headstock and use a pencil to mark the width you want.

Clamp the tube down and use a hand saw to cut.

While still clamped you can drill the holes for the wood screws.

Place the string retainer a short distance from the Nut.

Use a smaller bit to pre drill the holes for the wood screws.

Once you are ready to string the instrument simply slide the strings under the retainer.

It only needs to be low enough to make the strings sit properly on the nut.

Tailpiece, Bridge & Final Assembly

The tailpiece for this instrument was made with an old, steel shoe horn. I changed the direction of its bend by placing it in a vise and pushing it over. You could easily cut a piece of sheet metal for the tailpiece.

I drilled four holes for the strings to pass through.

It is mounted to the base of the neck with a wood screw and a common electric guitar strap button.

See page 171-176 for more about tailpiece's

The neck is secured to the body with a wood screw by
drilling a small hole in flaps that were cut in the hubcap.

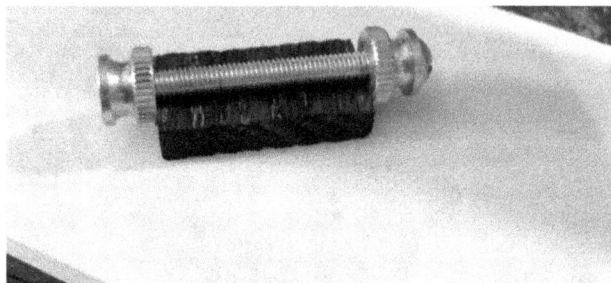

The bridge is a small piece of oak and a brass bolt.

This is a floating type bridge and is held in place by the tension of the strings.

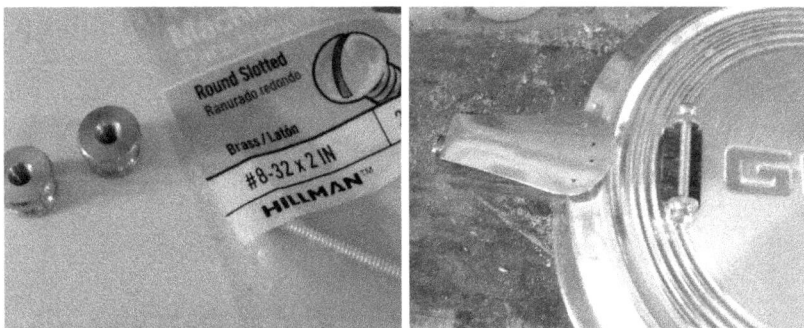

See page 171-176 for more about bridges

Put the strings on, tune it and then get the music flowing.

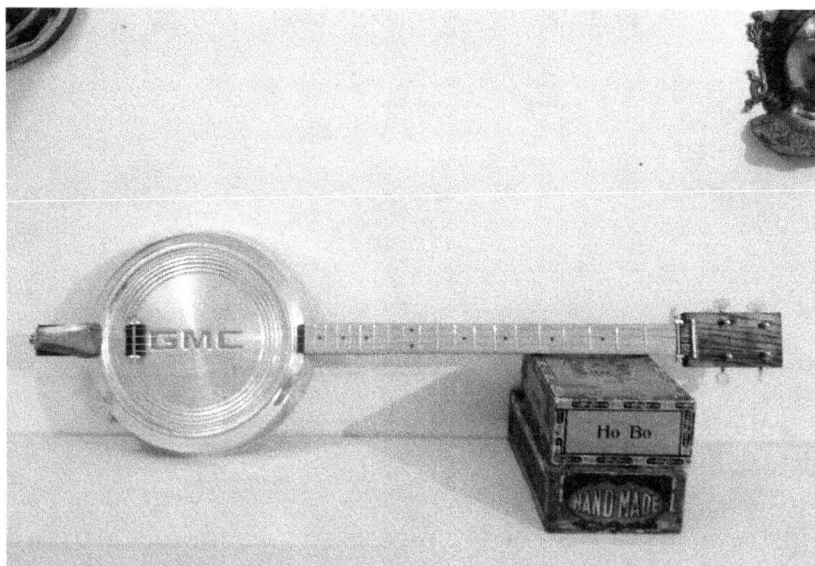

The completed Tenor Hubcap Banjo.

Headstock's

This section has been added to show examples of different headstock designs.

The instruments headstock is a nice sized area for folk artist's to take advantage of.

Jack Daniel's Whiskey Barrel headstock.

A traditional acoustic headstock drilled out with a Forstner bit and a dremel sander.

Art Deco

Paddle Board

One string Diddley Bow with violin type carving.

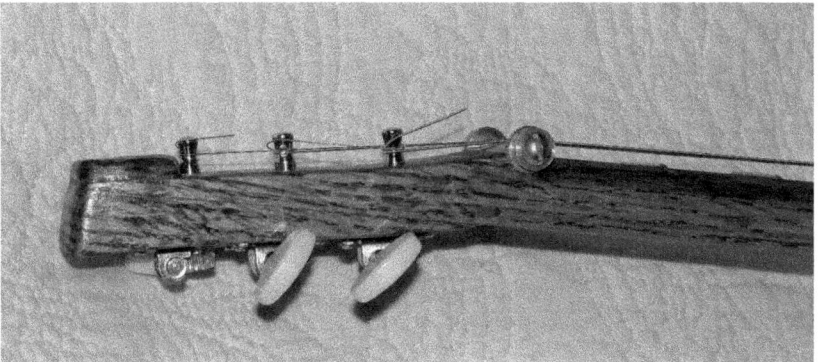

Three string with scarf joint.

This headstock was made by cutting various sized pieces of dowel and then gluing them together.

Strat style headstock with accent piece.

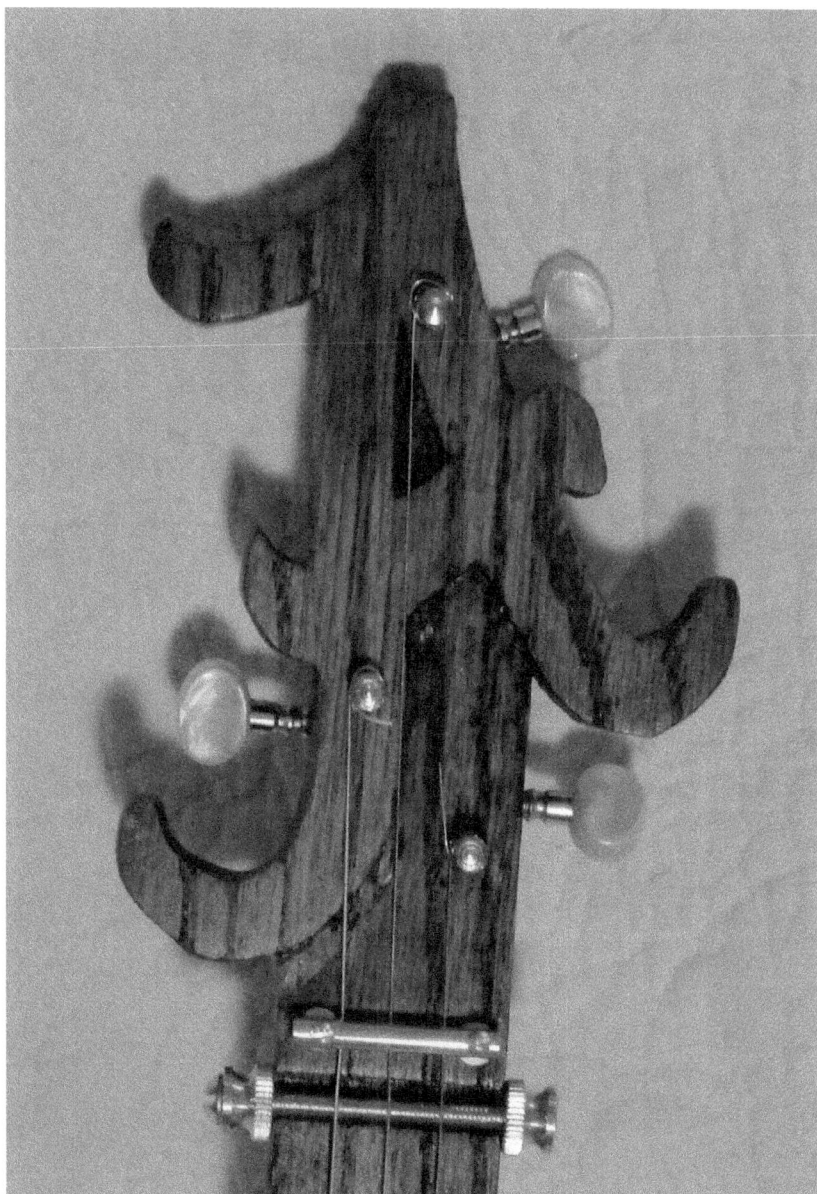

This headstock was lettered by using a bandsaw and a dremel.

Owl headstock carved using Dremel carving tools

Kalimba (Thumb Piano)

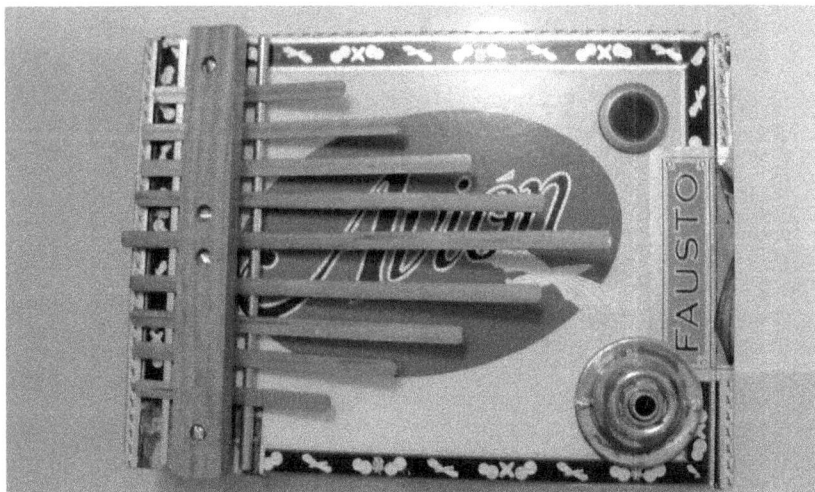

Thumb pianos have been around, in some form or fashion, for several thousand years.

The instrument is intended to be hand held and the tines are plucked with the thumbs.

These instruments were originally made using gourds for the body. The nice thing about this instrument is you can utilize just about anything for the body including wood, a cigar box, a vintage lunchbox, a sardine can etc..

The Kalimba is a simple and inexpensive instrument to build.

The example that I built for this book has a jack and Piezo pickup. An electric Kalimba is in no way the norm. A sound hole or two is all that is needed but if you really want to rock the house, go ahead and add the pickup.

The tines will be made by cutting different lengths of steel. I use the steel from a roll of sink cleaner that can be purchased at any hardware store, costing about seven dollars for twenty feet of 1/4 inch width steel.

I'll be using 9 tines, 2 of each length except for the center.

2 tines - 2 and 3/4 inches
2 tines - 3 and 1/2 inches
2 tines - 4 and 3/4 inches
2 tines - 5 and 1/2 inches
1 tine - 6 inches

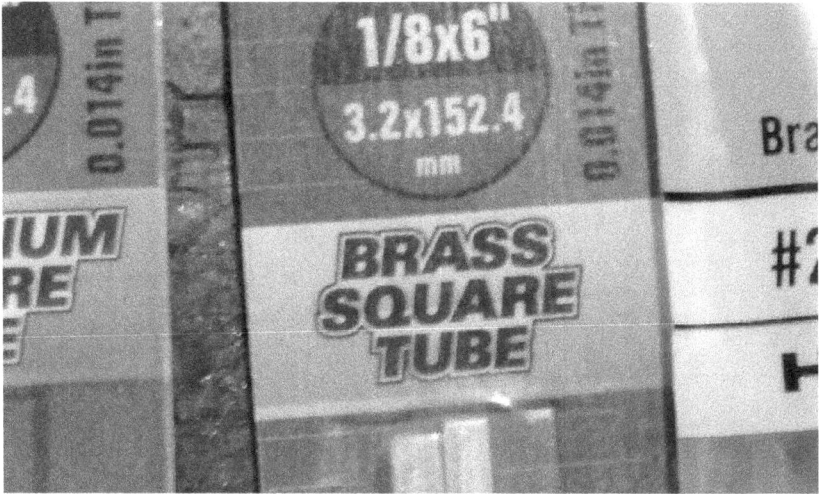

I will use two pieces of brass tubing for the tines to rest upon.

Two strips of oak about a half inch wide and their length should be just shy of the width of the box.

The picture above shows how the top pieces will be laid out. Nothing is attached yet. I'm just laying things out to help determine where the oak strip will be mounted underneath the lid.

Lay the tines down and mark where the mounting screws will go.

This shows the inside of the lid. Using wood glue, attach the oak strip.

Drill the holes for the mounting screws. One on each end and one on either side of the middle tine.

Once the glue on the strip under the lid has dried, pre drill the holes for the wood screws. Use a drill bit 1 size smaller than your screws. Lay the tines in place then lightly tighten the screws.

The brass pieces are not secured to the box. They are held in place by the tension of the tines once the screws are tightened.

The wood screws should be on the sides of the tines and never through them.

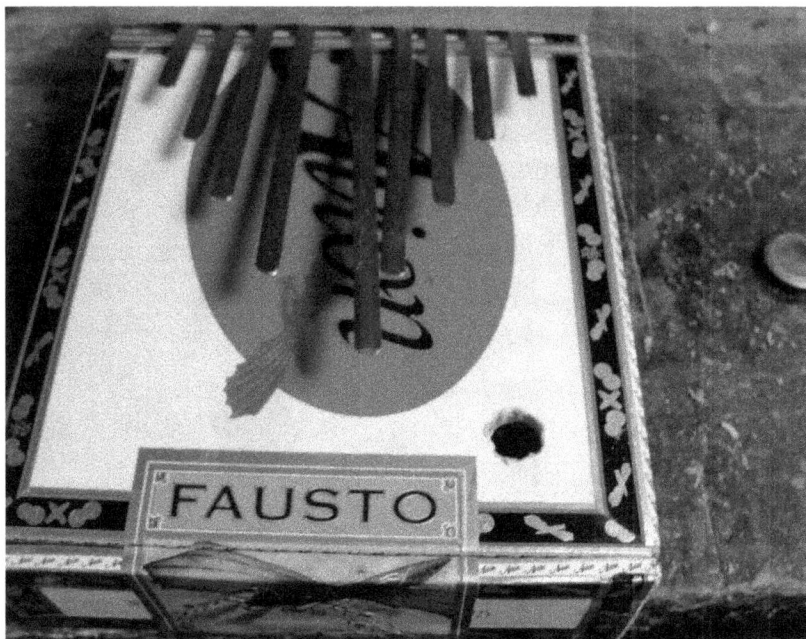

Drill a sound hole.

Drill a hole for the 1/4 jack

Optional: Insert a decorative grommet in the sound hole. Screened grommets can be purchased from CBGitty.com Plain grommets can be purchased at any hardware store.

Use an adhesive to mount the Piezo pickup inside the lid near the middle of the wood support.
I recommend Gorilla glue as the adhesive with a piece of masking tape holding it in place while the glue cures.

The jack cover is an old brass doorbell buzzer. Try to incorporate something recycled in all of your builds.

The tines should be tuned by moving them in or out. Loosen the screws just enough to move the tine to the position you need it. Keep in mind that this instrument was originally used to assist in telling stories and poems and the tuning was simply whatever helped the storyteller convey an emotion.

Experiment with different tine lengths. It's not uncommon to find one "odd" tuned tine on traditional antique Kalimba's.

Break all of the rules whenever possible.

Bracing

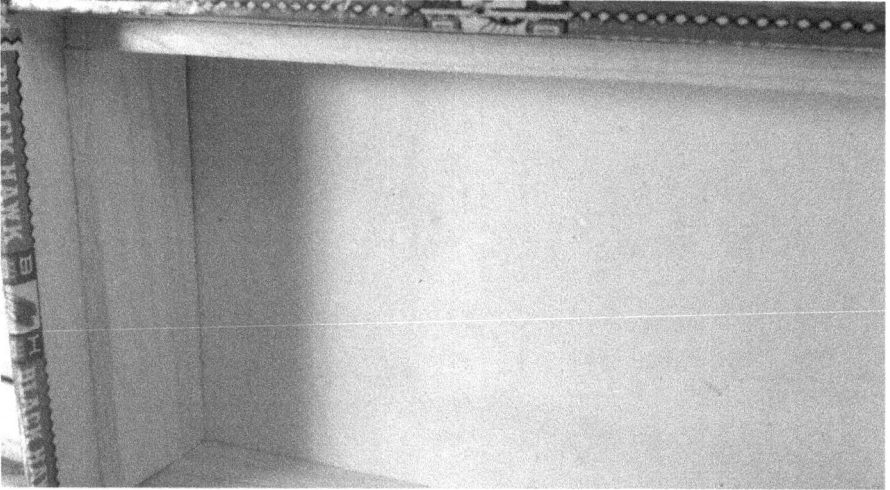

Both the structure and tone of an acoustic guitar can be enhanced with bracing. However, the cigar box guitar builder is primarily concerned with structural integrity. Try to give only as much bracing as is absolutely necessary. Older and more frail boxes should get more bracing. Adding thin strips of pine to cardboard cigar boxes makes them more viable for practical use as well. I've made numerous guitars out of cardboard cigar boxes using this method and they resonate extremely well.

Wind Your Own Pickups

In this section you will learn how to make an electric pickup.

This example is for a 3 string instrument but the same concept applies regardless of the number of strings.

We will be utilizing the lid of the instrument as the pickups housing.

The first step is to mark the box indicating where each string will run.

Drill a hole for each string and insert a small bolt.

You will need some very thin enamel coated wire. 42 or 43 gauge is preferable.

You will also need a standard, rectangular magnet and electrical tape.

The picture above shows the bolts as they come through the lid as well as the neck of the instrument. Use nuts to secure them in place.

Place the magnet against the bolts and use a small piece of electrical tape to wrap around and hold it in place.

This is a "neck through body" style guitar and I drilled through the neck to mount the bolts. These bolt's are what would be called the poles on a standard pickup. Therefore this is a 3 pole pickup.

Next, take the enamel wire and roll up a couple of inches and tape it to the lid of the box. Later it will become one of the connectors that you use to wire to the 1/4 jack.

With the end taped down, begin winding the wire tightly around the magnet.

It's going to take a lot of wraps. A store bought single coil pickup typically has over a thousand turns of wire so just keep that in mind.

Once you are satisfied with the number of wraps, take another few inches of the wire before you cut it from the roll and tape this down on the lid as well. This will be the other connector that goes to the 1/4 jack.

Now go ahead and wrap your magnet and wire with electrical tape very tightly.

Experiment with the number of turns of wire that you use.

The pickup itself is now complete. Next, connect it to the 1/4 jack.

I use a few inches of insulated wire to solder to the 1/4 jack and then I solder that wire to the enamel wire from my pickup.

Before you can solder the wire from the pickup you will need to remove the enamel coating.

Take the wires that you previously taped to the lid. Each wire needs enough enamel removed for the solder.

The wire is extremely thin so don't try and scrape the enamel off with a knife or razor, you will most likely just end up breaking the wire. Use a lighter or a match to quickly burn the enamel off. It only takes a second or so, then wipe them off and solder.

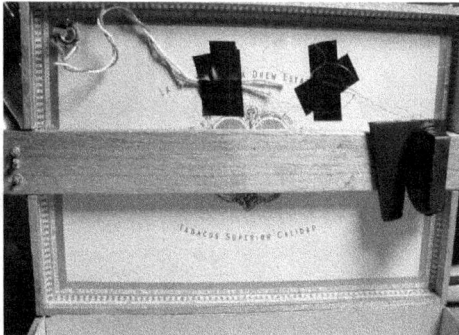

The picture above shows a completed pickup wired to a 1/4 jack. Tape the wires down to prevent them from bouncing around inside the box.

I prefer to purchase long neck 1/4 jacks because the typical thickness of cigar boxes can make installing a standard jack very cumbersome.

Wiring

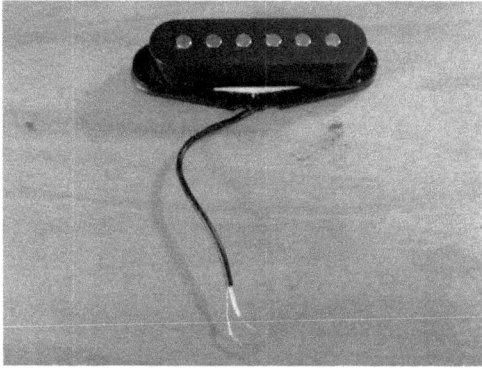

This section deals with basic wiring. I will demonstrate how to wire a single coil pickup to a volume knob and a 1/4 mono jack. A Piezo pickup can be substituted for the single coil pickup if desired.

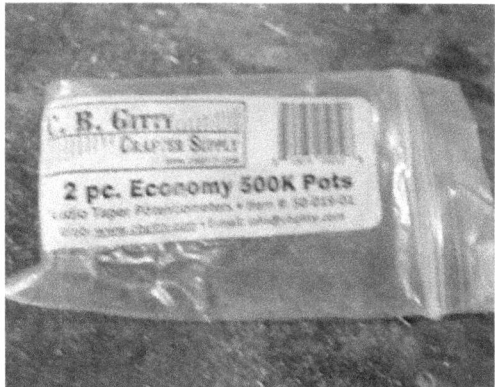

The volume knob is a 500k potentiometer.

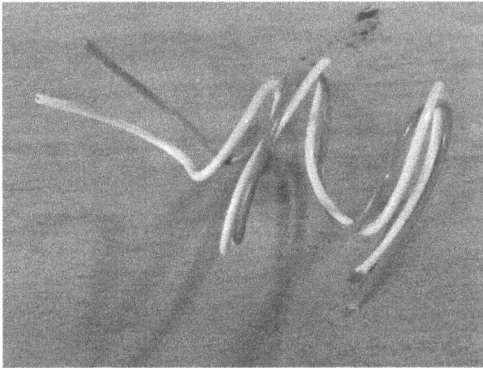

I keep a large roll of 20 gauge bell wire in my shop that I use for all of my instrument wiring.

Cut a length that is only slightly longer than what is needed for the instrument.

After cutting the length of wire, solder a piece to each connection from the pickup.

Most pickups will have a white and a black wire or a white and a braided wire. Bell wire is red and white so solder white to white and red to either black or the braid. It pays to be consistent. Once you begin wiring multiple pickups and switches you will understand why.

The white connection is made to the end post of the potentiometer.

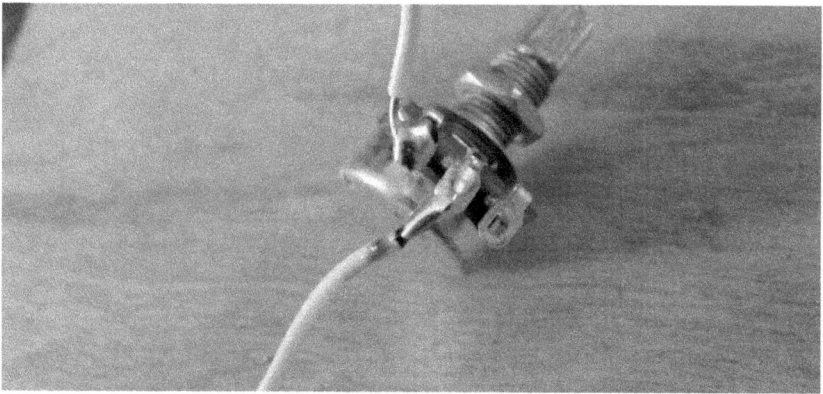

An additional white wire is soldered to the middle post.

This additional wire will go to the 1/4 jack.

The connection to the 1/4 jack.

Solder a piece of red wire to the other post of the 1/4 jack **but do not connect it to anything yet**.

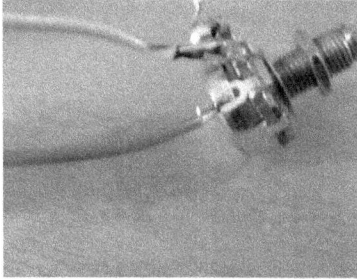

The red wire from the pickup is now placed on the remaining post. Before you solder, add another small piece of red red wire. See below.

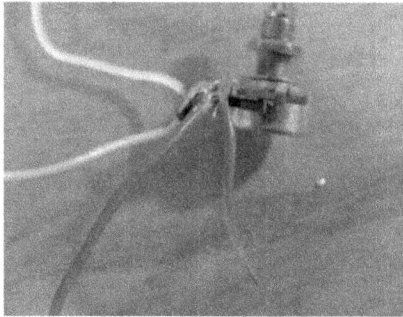

Connect this small piece of red wire to the red wire you soldered to the 1/4 jack earlier.

Now this connection will be soldered to the back of the potentiometer.

It may seem odd at first but it is very common for the back of the volume potentiometer to be used as a soldering point especially for ground connections. If you have trouble getting the solder to stick then try roughing up the back a little with some sandpaper. Also, never underestimate the need for a good soldering gun. The last thing you want is to have to open an instrument back up just to fix a faulty connection.

Once all the connections are soldered, you should plug it in and test it out. I keep a small battery powered amp in my shop just to test my wiring.

As you progress to more advanced wiring you may want to invest in some alligator test leads. They make it really easy to test everything before you solder. These are invaluable when you start wiring multiple pickups with tone knobs and switches. There are many great resources on the internet for wiring. Seymour Duncan has an example for pretty much any combination you can think of.

http://www.seymourduncan.com/support/wiring-diagrams/

Alligator Test Leads

Scarf Joint

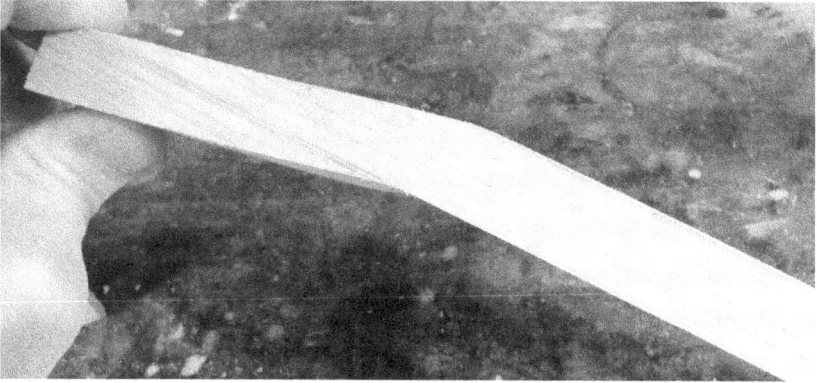

A scarf joint is merely a method of joining two pieces of wood together. For instrument builders it is a method to join two pieces of wood to create a slight angle at the headstock. The reason for this is to allow the tuners and the headstock to sit a bit lower than the nut. This eliminates the need for a string retainer.
(See page 123-126 for more about string retainers)

Flat neck and headstock with a string retainer.

Take the wood you will be using for the neck and sit it on its side. Use a straight edge to mark the line for your cut. Guitar scarf joints are typically between 10 and 15 degrees. Try and make the bend very slight. Only enough to eliminate the string retainer.

Start marking in the area just above where the Nut will be and run a line to the end of the board. Some builders cut short lines which makes the bend dramatic. Not only does this approach look odd but it leaves little area for the wood to bond and creates a weaker joint.

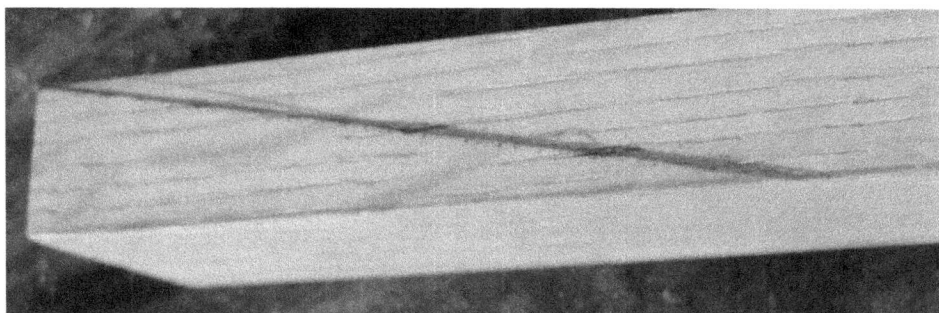

Here is the edge of a neck with the line drawn.

Use a band saw or hand saw to make the cut. Don't worry too much if your cut is not perfectly straight. You can smooth these areas later. The outside edges of the board, the areas we did not cut, are actually the areas that will be glued together.

Pick up the piece you cut off and move it to the other side of the board.

The glue will go between these two pieces. Notice that there is a great deal of wood that will be bonded together and the tuners will go through these two pieces which will also hold the two sections together. You won't have to worry about this coming apart.

Before you glue anything together, take the time to clean up your cut.

Using a belt sander is a good way to smooth off the rough areas that the band saw may have left behind.

Apply good wood glue. I prefer Titebond.

Use clamps to hold the two pieces firmly together. Wipe away any excess glue that gets squeezed out. Allow the glue to dry completely. The scarf joint is now complete.

Bridges and Tailpiece's

This section is intended to provide examples of a few different bridges and tailpiece designs.

This is one area of homemade instrument building that you can run the gamut of creativity from either purely functional to super awesome.

The key things to keep in mind are strength of the materials, string distance, string height and point of contact.

Many builders use door hinges, belt buckles, ammunition casings, small pieces of antler, box end wrenches, skeleton keys... The possibilities are endless.

Your individual artistic vision will take you down your own path.

This is a simple bridge constructed of scrap wood and a piece of fret wire. As stated before the point of contact with the string should be small.

Make sure the bridge lays flush with your instrument's body and that the height will be acceptable for your instrument's strings and frets.

A new four string tailpiece purchased on eBay.

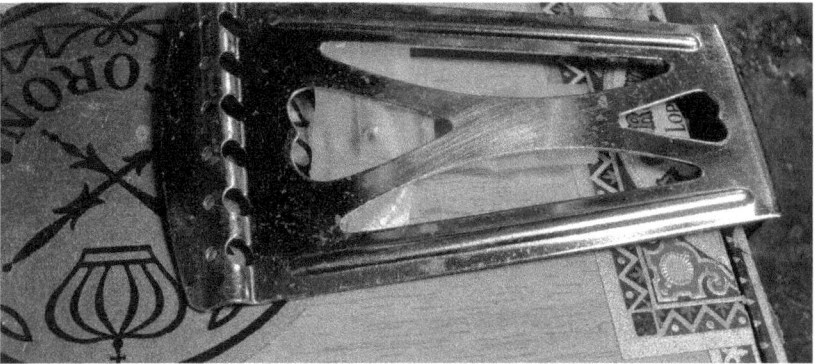

A rescued, vintage, six string tailpiece.

These types of tailpieces are not always the best option for homemade instruments. Often they are made for archtop guitars that likely have higher fretboards, higher bridges and radiused necks. Also, their length can be a hindrance especially if you are using cigar boxes which are typically less than 10 inches long.

These are all things that you can certainly work around but they warrant keeping in mind.

Tenor Banjo bridge.

Ukulele bridge.

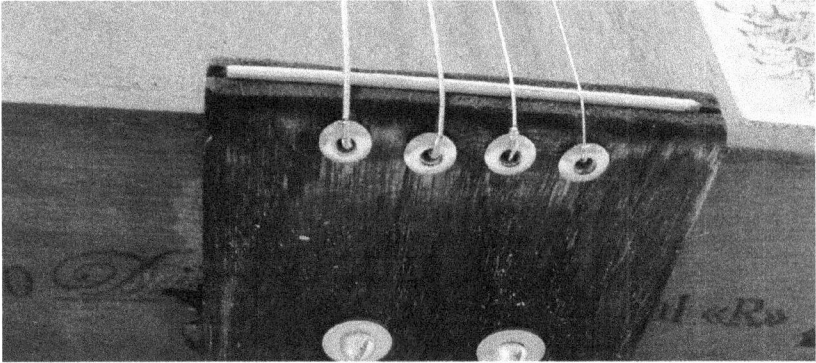

Pictured above is a bridge/tailpiece combo that I use quite often. This is especially beneficial for shorter instrument bodies.

It is similar to the bridge shown in this book for the relic 4 string, except this tailpiece is fretted on top and the strings are wrapped over.

The Piezo pickup is mounted to the other side of the tailpiece rather than on the instruments lid.

The picture below is a three string version with notches instead of a fret wire. This was a fretless guitar that I wanted to have an old school feel.

Build a wooden cigar bridge

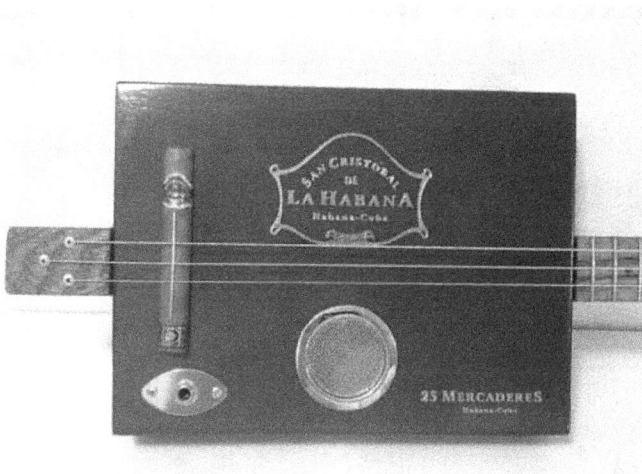

If the body of the instrument is a cigar box then why not make a bridge that looks like a cigar?

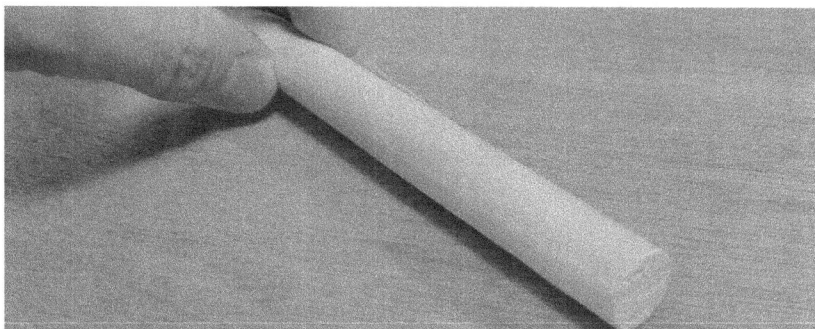

Start with a wooden dowel.

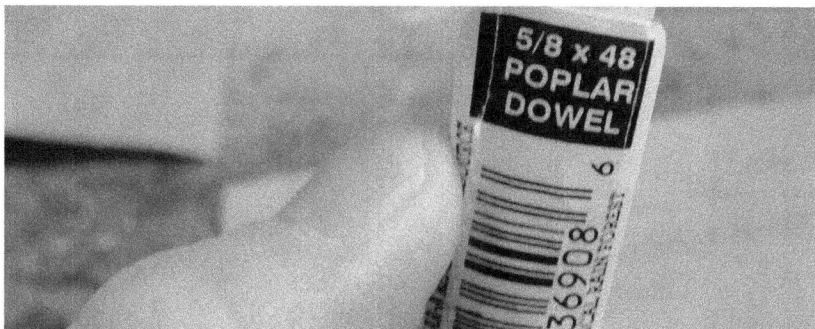

Use a 5/8 poplar or oak wooden dowel.

Using a band saw or hand saw, cut the dowel to the height you want.

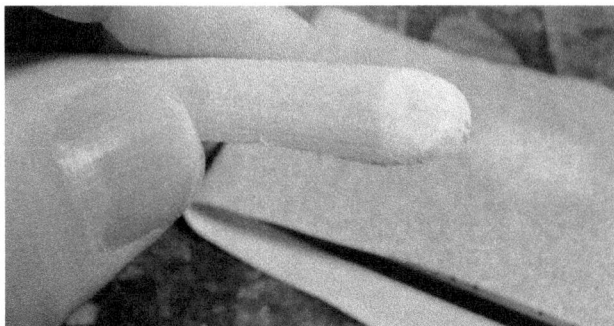

Use sand paper to give one end a slight curve.

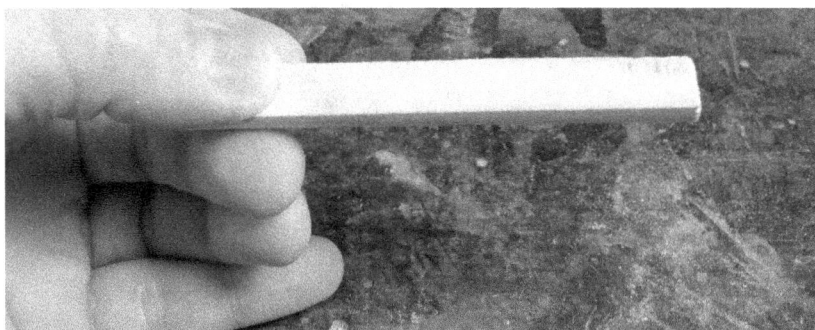

Lay it down on sand paper and run it back and forth or use a belt sander to make sure the bottom is completely flat.

The overall length of the bridge is up to you. I have mine just long enough for me to install a fret on top of it that will accommodate the number of strings on the instrument and also be sure to leave enough room for a cigar band.

Get a brown paper lunch sack.

Cut it into strips. Uneven widths are best.

Take the cut pieces and crumple them up.

The crinkles really give it the look of tobacco leaves.

Using the fret saw, cut a fret slot on the top of the dowel.

I get the cut started then flip the saw over and run the dowel back and forth to finish the cut. Be careful making this cut. Watch your fingers.

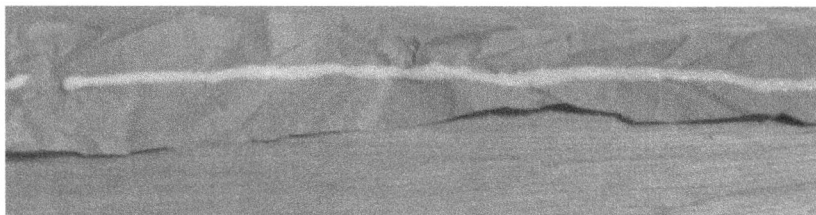

Run a bead of wood glue on a strip.

Don't use any more glue than necessary. Any excess glue that squeezes out should be wiped away quickly, especially if you plan to stain the wrapper. The stain will not adhere properly to any area that has glue on it.

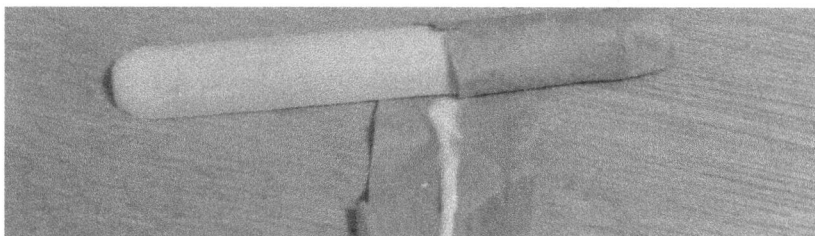

Start at one end and begin wrapping.

Two or three strips is usually enough to wrap the wood. Jagged edges just make it look more authentic. You may need an extra dab of glue on the ends.

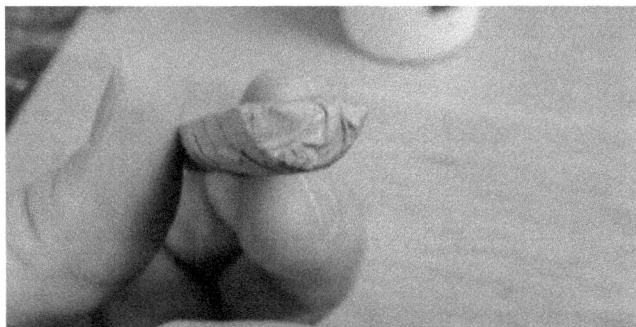

Make sure everything is wrapped tightly and excess glue is wiped away.

Using an exacto knife, cut through the paper to open the area that was sawed earlier. Only cut enough for the length of the fret wire you will install.

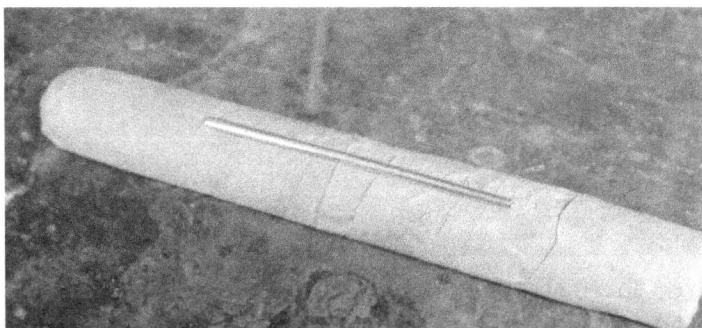

Cut the fret wire and tap it and/or press it in place.

You can leave it the color it is and maybe add some polyurethane. For a darker look add stain.

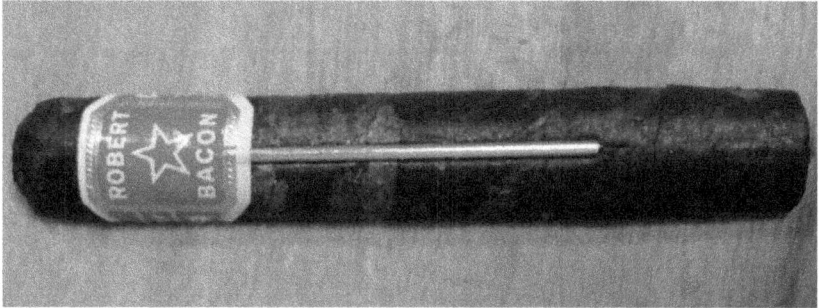

You can also add a cigar band now if you want. It goes on the end that was slightly rounded.

Here are two finished wooden cigar bridges. One is fretted one is not. One is natural color and one is stained.

Cajón Drum

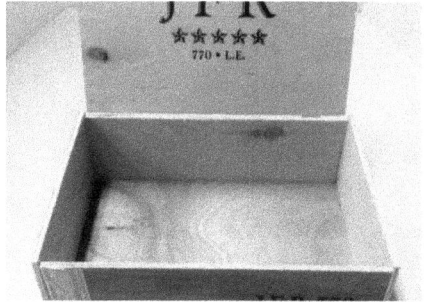

The Cajón drum is amazingly simple to make and they sound great. This instrument is believed to have originated in Peru sometime in the late 18th century.

I've seen a few street performers that have added a pedal from a bass drum to their Cajón to allow them to play guitar and sing while their foot beats the drum.

When using your hands, the Cajón can replicate both snare and bass drum tones. With practice you can replicate even more percussion tones. The Cajón is sometimes, and for good reason, referred to as a drum kit in a box.

You can use any number of materials to build your Cajón drum; Plywood, desk drawer, shipping crate, wine box etc..

I do recommend though that whatever you construct your Cajón from that you use a fairly thin wood for the area that the snares will sit on. Too thick and the tone could be diminished and/or you may also have to strike it harder.

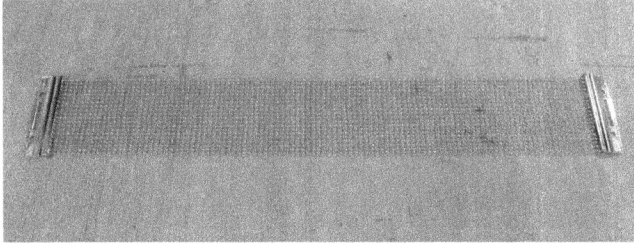

For this instrument we need a snare. I purchased this replacement snare on eBay.

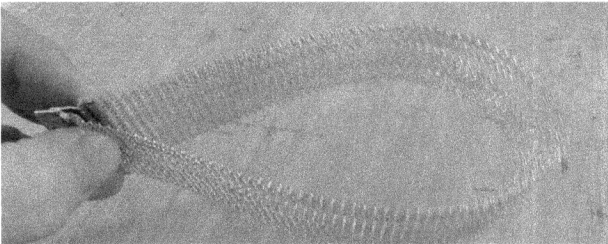

Find the center by bending the snare over.

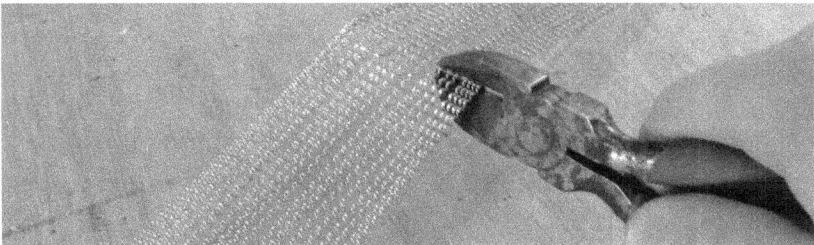

Use wire cutters to snip the snare in half.

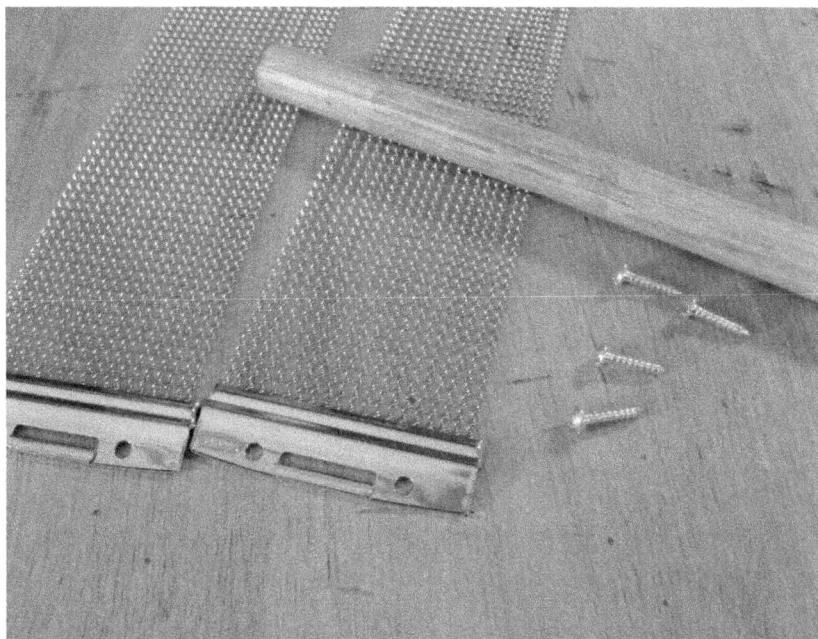

Cut a wooden dowel to the width of the box you will be using.

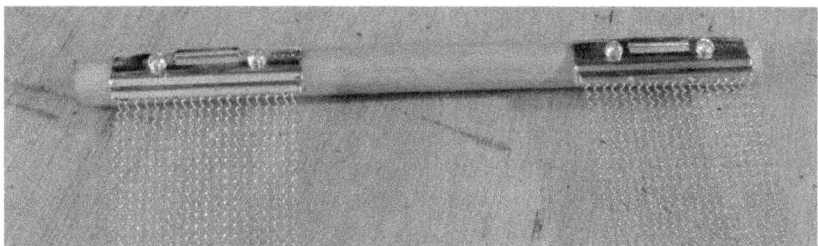

Attach the snare's to the dowel using wood screws.

Wood screws will go through the box on each side and into the wooden dowel. Make sure the dowel is rotated to where it places a good deal of tension on the snares.

Shown above is the wood screw on one side that secures the dowel. You can also place a screw in the middle of the dowel to ensure it does not rotate and lose tension.

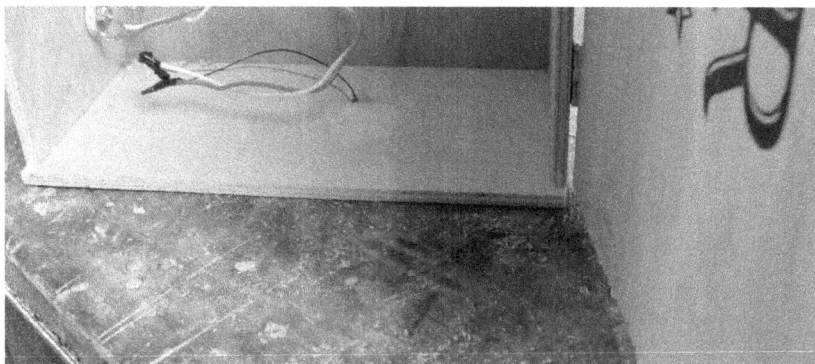

Add a Piezo pickup and a 1/4 Jack. In this example I placed the Piezo on the side wall opposite of the dowel. This provides cleaner bass tones when I tap the walls.

Experiment with Piezo placement as well as the number of Piezo's in your instrument.

A sound hole can be drilled into the box as well but not on the side with the snares. The size of the sound hole is something you should experiment with as well. I typically don't put a sound hole on this size of an electric Cajón. When using wine or larger cheese boxes I will use a hole from 1 to 3 inches in size.

Use wood glue to seal the box shut.

Now you are ready to play the Cajón. Your hands are in essence the drumsticks. One hand should slap or tap the area where the snare is installed and the other hand can tap the top or sides to produce other tones.

Washtub Bass (Gutbucket)

I can't think of any instrument better suited to accompany a Cigar Box Guitar than a Washtub Bass. Often referred to as a Gutbucket, this instrument brings to mind visions of bluegrass and mountain musicians.

The metal tub itself is the instrument's resonator and the deep, loud bass tones generally come from the larger tubs. However, I have seen and heard some really good examples built with mid-sized, plastic buckets similar to what you might use to wash your car.

There are numerous varieties but I am going to show you how to construct what I feel to be the most common.

Galvanized steel tub 10 gallons or larger
Eye bolt - optional, could just run rope through the tub
Resonator hole or raise one side with a block of wood
Pole or board
Rope, heavy gauge wire or an actual standup bass string

If you plan on using a used tub be sure it is structurally sound. Some rust is ok but if you can see light through it then it's probably not viable.

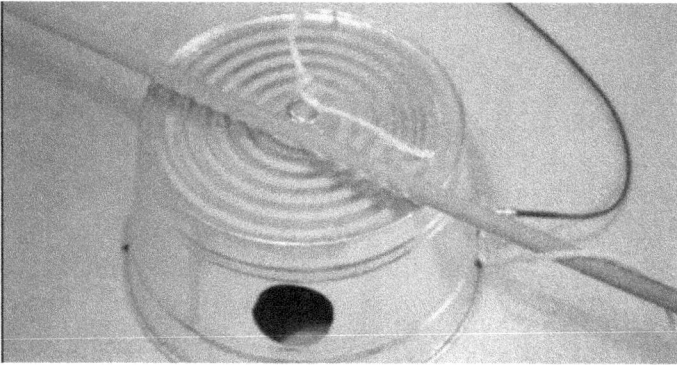

The Washtub bass is comprised of very few parts. In fact all you really need is a washtub, a piece of rope and a broom handle.

The example shown above has a few extra's such as a Piezo pickup, an eyebolt and a soundhole.

Many people forego the eyebolt and simply run the rope through the washtub and put a knot in it. This actually works really well and resonates just as well if not slightly better than the eyebolt method.

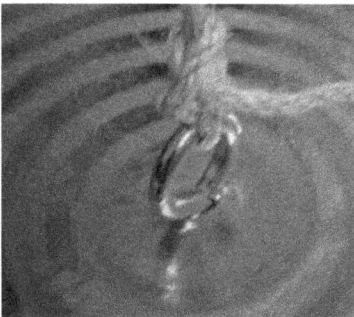

I like the eyebolt because it allows me to quickly change to a different size rope. I like to experiment with different width rope as well a wire and other materials as the "string" of the instrument.

Drill a hole through the center of the washtub either large enough for the eyebolt or the rope you will be using.

I use a 1/4 inch piece of oak inside of the washtub for the eyebolt to run through. It server two purposes. One, is to apply surface tension to the washtub to allow the tub to resonate better. Two, it provides me with a good surface to attach the Piezo pickup to. Mounting the pickup directly to the washtub can provide a very undesirable tinny sound to the instrument.

Mount the Piezo using basically the same method utilized for the Hubcap instrument on **Page 118-122**
The Piezo is mounted within a small piece of wood which is then attached to the oak board using wood screws.

Drill a hole in the side of the bucket for the 1/4 jack.

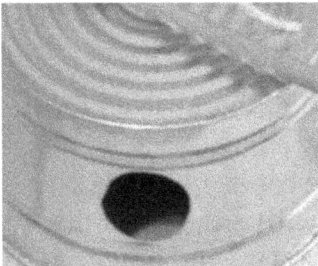

You can put a sound hole in this instrument for times when it is not amplified. Another method to get more sound is to prop one side of the tub up on a block of wood. I used a hole saw mounted in a hand drill and had someone hold the tub while I drilled. Once drilled I used a file to smooth the opening.

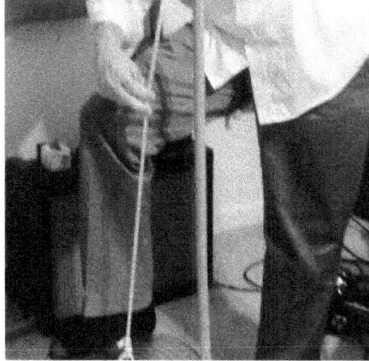

The handle I used for my washtub bass is a wooden push pole used for navigating shallow river beds. Many other items could be used such as a broom handle or a shovel handle. Many people just use a 1 X 2 piece of oak.

The height is something you may want to experiment with. I prefer lengths of about 4 to 5 feet.

All that is required to connect the string to the board is a hole large enough for the rope to pass through. A simple knot holds it in place.

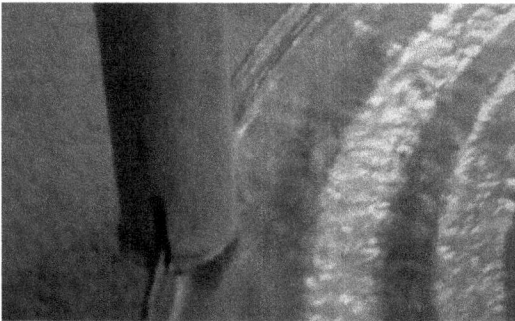

To keep the board in place you will want to cut a notch so that the rim on the bottom of the washtub will fit inside of it.

To play the instrument, place a foot on the tub and then put varying amounts of tension, by pulling and releasing on the pole, while plucking the rope.

You can also grip the rope in various positions to alter the tone.

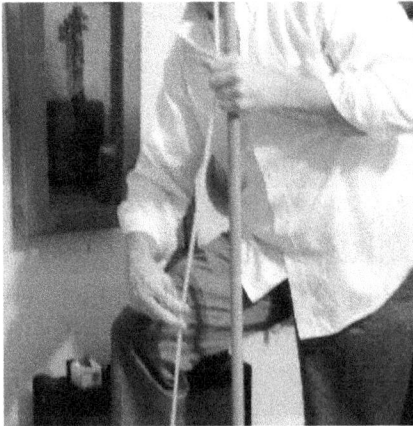

Recommended resources:

C. B. Gitty: cbgitty.com

MRWS Instruments: mrwsinstruments.com parts supplier in Australia

Stewart-MacDonald: stewmac.com

Rockler Woodworking: rockler.com

For instructional videos for playing Cigar Box instruments visit: rootsmusicschool.com

While you are at it, stop by my place: CharlesAtchison.com

Also on face book: Facebook.com/CharlesAtchisonFolkArtisan

This guitar is a combination of several elements explained within this book. It is a Cajon drum, a Kalimba and an electric 4 string guitar. A band in a box.

CharlesAtchison.com

CHARLES ATCHISON
FOLK ARTISAN
Hand Made

THUNDER LIGHTNING

TM

RESONATING CONES

HAND SPUN, HIGH QUALITY, ALUMINUM RESONATING CONES
DESIGNED TO ENHANCE BOTH THE VOLUME AND TONE OF CIGAR BOX GUITARS

WWW.CHARLESATCHISON.COM

Take your builds to the next level with a
quality hand spun aluminum resonator cone.
Available in 2 sizes, designed specifically for
Cigar Box Guitars.

CharlesAtchison.com